Contents

To the student

This book will help you to learn new English words while having fun at the same time. Many of the tests use pictures – such as the tests on things in the home, food and drink, fruit and vegetables, sports equipment and clothes. Others are based on word types – for example, verbs, adjectives, prepositions and adverbs. There are also tests on pairs of words that have similar meanings, opposites, and words that people often mix up. Use the contents list to find the right test for you. Or go through the book and choose one that looks interesting or has drawings that you like. So if you feel like doing a crossword, choose a crossword. If you feel like looking at cartoons, try one of the *Phrases* tests where you match words to a picture. If a test is fun to do, this is one of the best ways of learning new words fast. There's no need to start at the beginning and work through every test in the book. The tests at the end are no more difficult than the ones at the beginning.

There are tip boxes on nearly every page. They will give you extra help and information. They will also give you ideas on how to learn new words.

To really **learn** a new word, you will need to do each test more than once. So use a pencil to write the answers in the book when you test yourself. Then, check your answers and look carefully at the words you didn't know or got wrong. Finally, rub out your answers ready for the next time you try that test. Each test will take you between five and fifteen minutes the first time you do it, but the next time you will probably be much quicker.

The tests in this book do not get harder as you go from Test 1 to Test 60. However, the five books in the Test Your Vocabulary series are carefully graded from Book 1 (for beginners) to Book 5, which is for advanced students. If you find this book is too easy, try the next one up. If you find it is too hard, try the next one down.

Good luck with learning the words in this book. And we hope that you will enjoy using the words in real situations once you've learnt them here.

Peter Watcyn Jones and Olivia Johnston

1 Things in the home

Write the numbers 1 to 12 next to the correct words.

blender _4_

bottle opener ___

briefcase ___

broom ___

coat hanger ___

dustpan ___

light bulb ___

pepper grinder ___

potato peeler ___

suitcase ___

tea towel ___

tray ___

- A *tea towel* is something we use to dry the dishes after we have done the washing-up. In American English it is called a *dish cloth*.

- All but three of the items on this page are compound nouns. Some compound nouns are written as one word like *briefcase*, *suitcase* and *dustpan*. Some are written as two words like *bottle opener* and *tea towel*. Can you think of another compound noun ending with the word ... *opener* and another one ending with the word ... *towel*?

2 Adjectives: people 1

The adjectives in the box below are all in the crossword. Read the clues and complete the crossword with them.

brave	generous	grateful	honest	independent	jealous
lively	mature	miserable	patient	popular	proud
relaxed	reliable	sensible	superficial	warm	weird

Across

1 She doesn't think about anything seriously or have any deep feelings. She's so _____

6 He's always _____. He's never in a hurry and he's always calm.

8 She's the most _____ person in the school. Everybody likes her.

10 He's very _____. If he says he'll do something, then he does it.

13 She's very _____. She never complains about the pain she is in all the time.

14 She always tells the truth. She's very _____

15 He's a very _____ teacher. He doesn't get cross even when he has to repeat something three times.

17 They were very _____ when we said they could stay in our house while we were away.

Down

1 He never drinks and drives. He's too _____ to do something silly like that.

2 She's going to travel around the world for six months on her own. She must be very _____

3 She always has fun at parties because she's so bright and _____

4 He never smiles and always looks _____. I don't know what his problem is.

5 She's only seventeen but she seems much older. She's very _____ for her age.

7	He makes her _____ when he looks at other girls.
9	She looks _____. Why does she always wear such strange clothes?
11	They're very rich but they are also really _____ with their money. They give wonderful presents.
12	He got 100% in all his exams. His parents are really _____ of him.
16	She's always _____ and friendly. You always feel welcome at her house.

 The word *sensible* may be a 'false friend' for many students of English whose mother tongue has Latin roots. In English, *sensible* means *clever in a practical way*.
She won't take any silly risks. She's a sensible girl.
It does not mean the same as *sensitive*, which means *easily hurt* or *delicate*.
She can't use soap on her face. She's got very sensitive skin.
Don't tease him. He's very sensitive and you might make him cry.

3 Phrasal verbs 1

Complete each sentence with a phrasal verb in the correct tense. Sometimes you will have to separate the verb from the particle.

blow up	break down	bring up	cut down	~~get over~~	hang up
keep on	knock out	let down	pick up	put off	put out
ring off	run out of	set out	show off	take off	tell off	turn up

1   Have you __got over__ that terrible cough you had last time I saw you?

2   He touched one of the sculptures in the exhibition, and the guard saw him and _____ him _____.

3   Her car _____ petrol and she had to hitchhike to a petrol station.

4   Her husband left her when the children were babies and she _____ them _____ herself.

5   I know you don't want to talk to Jenny but it's really important to do it today. You can't _____ it _____ any longer.

6   Jimmy's giving me a lift. He's _____ me _____ tomorrow morning at eleven.

7   My little sister often _____ when we have visitors. She wants to get more attention.

8   Our car _____ on the motorway and we had to call a garage to get it fixed.

9   Our plane _____ an hour late so we landed in Rome an hour later than we'd expected.

10 Please _____ your cigarette. Can't you see the 'no smoking' sign?

11   She _____ asking me for money so in the end I had to give her some.

12   Terrorists put a bomb under the bridge and _____ it _____.

13   The robber hit the bank manager over the head and _____ him _____. He was unconscious for half an hour.

14   Tony still hadn't arrived by ten. Eventually he _____ at 11.30 with two other people.

15   We _____ on our trip quite early but there was already a lot of traffic on the road.

16   We _____ the tree in the front of our house because we didn't get any light in our sitting room.

17   We promised to go and visit her tomorrow so we have to. We can't _____ her _____. She'd be so disappointed.

18   We were talking on the phone and suddenly she just _____. Maybe somebody rang at her front door.

The one-word synonym of to *get over* (an illness) is to *recover*. The one-word synonym of to *tell someone off* is to *admonish someone*. Phrasal verbs are more informal and much more common even in written English than their one-word synonyms.

Question: What's the difference between a nail and a boxer?
Answer: One gets knocked in and the other gets knocked out.

4 The body

Write the numbers 1 to 12 next to the correct words.

ankle __12__   chin _____   throat _____

bottom _____   elbow _____   thumb _____

cheek _____   lips _____   waist _____

chest _____   stomach _____   wrist _____

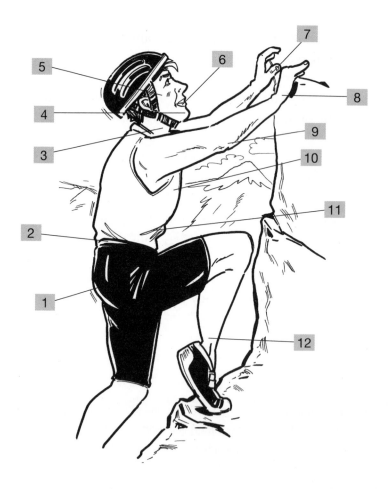

5 Food and drink 1

Match the pairs of adjectives on the left to the nouns on the right.

1	baked or mashed __k__	a	boiled eggs
2	fried or scrambled _____	b	bread
3	brown or white _____	c	cola
4	fried or grilled _____	d	chocolate
5	hard or soft _____	e	cream
6	hot or mild _____	f	curry
7	plain or milk _____	g	eggs
8	rare or medium _____	h	fish
9	regular or diet _____	i	milk
10	skimmed or full-cream _____	j	mineral water
11	single or double _____	k	potatoes
12	still or sparkling _____	l	tea
13	strong or weak _____	m	steak
14	sweet or dry _____	n	tomatoes
15	tinned or fresh _____	o	wine

We also talk about *black* or *white* tea and coffee, *red* or *white* wine and *strong* or *mild* cheese.

6 The house and garden

Write the numbers 1 to 16 next to the correct words.

branch _4_

burglar alarm _____

bush _____

chimney _____

door handle _____

dustbin _____

flowerpot _____

French windows _____

greenhouse _____

hedge _____

hose _____

lawn _____

letterbox _____

patio _____

satellite dish _____

tap _____

 In America, a garden is usually called a *yard*. In British English, the word *yard* is uncommon. It means a *small paved or concrete area at the back of the house*. The modern word for a paved area at the back of the house is a *patio*.

7 Adjectives: opposites

Match the adjectives in the box to their opposites. Then complete the sentences a) – j) with one of the adjectives on the page.

artificial	broad-minded	cautious	delicious	exciting	gentle
light-hearted	pessimistic	~~rational~~	sensitive	sudden	tiny
	uninterested	unlucky			

1 emotional   *rational*

2 gigantic   _____

3 real   _____

4 dull   _____

5 daring   _____

6 narrow-minded   _____

7 gradual   _____

8 keen   _____

9 lucky   _____

10 thick-skinned   _____

11 serious   _____

12 optimistic   _____

13 disgusting   _____

14 aggressive   _____

a   She's a very _emotional_ person. She's always laughing or crying or falling in love.

b   The food at the hotel was absolutely _____. None of us could eat it.

c   He is very _____. You can say anything and he won't be shocked.

d   He enjoys picking fights with people. He really is _____.

e   At first I didn't realise those roses were _____. I tried smelling one of them.

f   The improvement in his health was very _____. At first we didn't notice that he was getting better.

g   She's very _____. She's always cheerful and never gets depressed.

h   I wish I was more _____. I'd like to try surfing or going up in a hot air balloon but I'm too scared.

i   He's very _____. He always thinks something bad is going to happen to him.

j   She gets very upset if people don't like her paintings. She's terribly _____ about her work.

 Test 2 on pages 2–3 also practises adjectives. The Tip on page 3 explains the difference between *sensible* and *sensitive*.

8 Crime

Complete each sentence with the correct word from the box.

> bullies ~~burglar~~ dealers drink driving fine gangs
> graffiti hooligans judge mugged robbers
> shoplifting speeding theft violence

1   A _burglar_ broke into our house while we were away this weekend and stole our video.

2   Drug _____ who sell heroin to teenagers are among the worst kind of criminals.

3   Car _____ in this area is increasing. Fifty cars were stolen last week.

4   Fourteen football _____ were arrested after the match. They were fighting and throwing bottles onto the pitch.

5   He should have taken a taxi home after the party. He got stopped by the police and lost his licence for _____.

6   He was doing 80 kilometres an hour in the centre of town. He was caught _____ on a camera.

7   He's scared to walk home from school on his own because last week some _____ in the year above him broke his personal stereo.

8   If you park on a double yellow line, you might get a parking _____.

9   In court, the _____ said he should stay in prison for the rest of his life.

10 She was arrested for _____. She stole a pair of jeans and a sweater from a clothes shop.

11 Some people think that the _____ on TV and in films leads to crime.

12 The health centre wall has some big red _____ on it. They'll have to repaint the wall.

13 There was a big fight between two _____ of teenagers outside the club. Seventeen people were hurt.

14 Two armed bank _____ got away with £50,000 yesterday.

15 Two guys _____ a friend of mine recently and ran off with her handbag.

The words *robbers* and *rob* are usually used about banks, post offices and jewellery shops.

Robbers got away with £2 million from a high street bank yesterday.
Two armed men robbed a jewellery shop this morning.

When we speak about theft from a house, we usually use the words *burglars*, *burgle* and *break into*.

Question: Who are the strongest criminals in the world?
Answer: Shoplifters.

Question: What did the hooligan say after breaking all the windows?
Answer: I've had a smashing time.

9 Jobs

Complete the sentences with the correct words from the box.

astronaut	caretaker	cashier	chef	diver	driving instructor
engineer	estate agent	farmer	lawyer	lifeguard	~~model~~
	pilot	speech therapist	surgeon		

The group of people I was friendly with at college have all got very different jobs.

1   Elana is very beautiful and slim. You've probably seen her wearing expensive clothes on the covers of magazines. She's a __*model*__.

2   Naomi is a _____. She helps people who have problems speaking. Sometimes they've had an accident or an illness, and sometimes they were born with the problem.

3   Jo's a _____. He's got a lot of fruit trees and he also keeps sheep and cows.

4   Steve is a _____ in a bank. He loves counting money!

5   Tony looks after a big block of flats. He says being a _____ is great because he gets his own free flat with the job.

6   Sandra is always in her car. She's a _____. Everyone she teaches passes their test first time.

7   Rose is a _____. At the moment she flies a small plane from London to Paris three times a week.

8   Bob has the most unusual job. He's an _____. His ambition is to set up a new space station.

9   Tom is an _____. He helps people to buy and sell houses and flats.

10   Katie is a _____ in a big hotel. I've never eaten there but people say the food is amazing.

11   Alex repairs oil rigs underwater. He is a deep-sea _____.

12   Karen is a _____. She used to spend a lot of time in court but now she helps people sort out property and money when they get divorced.

13   Glenn is an _____ with a big telephone company. When people have problems with their phones, they call him.

14   I had to have an operation on my knee last year. My friend Luisa is a _____ at the Fleming Hospital and she did it.

15   Ben loves the sea. He owns a surfing shop and he also works as a _____ on a big beach in Cornwall. Last summer he saved a little boy from drowning.

Try consolidating your knowledge of jobs words by making an occupations word-web. Start like this:

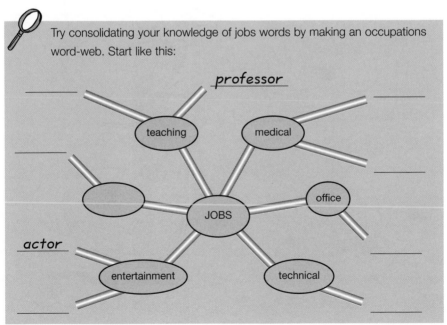

professor

teaching

medical

office

JOBS

actor

entertainment

technical

10 Food and drink 2

Write the numbers 1 to 12 next to the correct words.

beat __6__   roast _____

chop _____   slice _____

grate _____   spread _____

heat _____   squeeze _____

mix _____   stir _____

peel _____   whip _____

 Beating and *whipping* are very similar actions. We generally say *beat* for eggs and *whip* for cream.

Question: Why are cooks cruel?

Answer: Because they are always beating eggs and whipping cream.

11 Choose the word

Choose the word which best completes each sentence.

1 Anyone wanting to go to the meeting, please ___*put up*___ your hands.

   a) take up   (b) put up
   c) lift   d) rise

2 I have no brothers or sisters. I am _____ child.

   a) an only   b) one
   c) a unique   d) a single

3 I'm terribly sorry, I seem to have _____ my book at home.

   a) lost   b) forgotten
   c) left   d) hidden

4 My sister and I are always quarrelling. We just don't seem to _____.

   a) get off   b) get together
   c) get on   d) get by

5 A lot of single parents find it difficult to _____ their children and do a job.

   a) grow up   b) take up
   c) develop   d) bring up

6 We _____ to inform you that this flight will be delayed for five hours.

   a) sorry   b) regret
   c) apologise   d) pity

7   Everyone should _____ this charity. They're doing a lot of good work in developing countries.

a) agree   b) support

c) stand up   d) supply

---

8   I only paid £5 for this shirt. It was a real _____.

a) luck   b) sale

c) bargain   d) cheap

---

9   I always try to _____ something each month for my holidays.

a) save   b) spare

c) spend   d) put

---

10   I don't have a job. I'm _____.

a) lonely   b) sick

c) unused   d) unemployed

---

11   Juventus _____ AC Milan in the football final.

a) beat   b) won

c) passed   d) lost

---

12   The train now standing at _____ seven has just arrived from Brighton.

a) station   b) platform

c) lane   d) path

 If you make a lot of mistakes in this test, try writing sentences with the words that confused you. Then do the test again in a few days' time.

12 Fruit and vegetables

Write the numbers 1 to 14 next to the correct words.

aubergine __4__

broccoli _____

cabbage _____

cauliflower _____

cherry _____

coconut _____

courgette _____

cucumber _____

fig _____

onion _____

peach _____

pepper _____

plum _____

tangerine _____

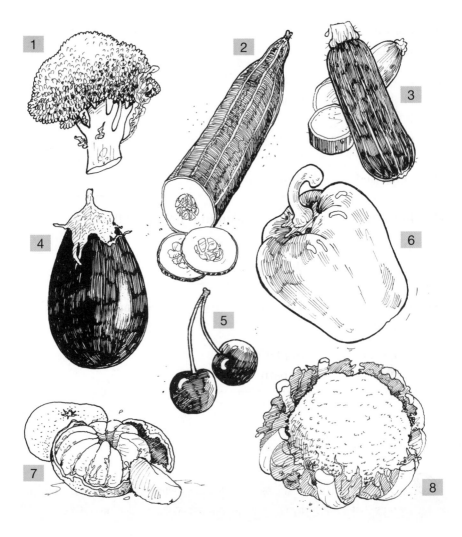

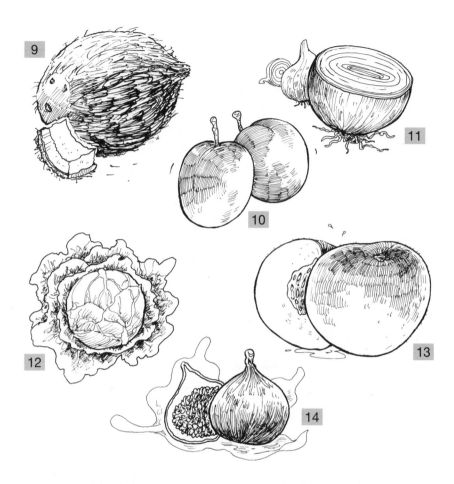

- There are lots of fruits similar to tangerines but which have different names, for example *clementines, mandarins, satsumas*. Most people don't know the difference between them and nobody really cares apart from greengrocers. The most useful general word for all of them is probably *tangerine*.

- On the night of Christmas Eve in Britain, children hang out a sock (called a stocking, for some reason at Christmas!) for Father Christmas to fill with presents while they are asleep. It's traditional for Father Christmas to put a tangerine and some nuts at the bottom of the stocking, in the toe. The tradition originates from the time when tangerines were luxuries.

13 Getting a job

Complete the conversation with the correct words from the box.

> advertisement ~~application form~~ career CV driving licence
> full-time interview offer organized part-time qualifications
> references sense of humour skills starting salary stressful
> temporary training course unemployed well-paid

A: Did you have to fill in an (1) _application form_ to get your job?

B: No. I saw an (2) _____ in the newspaper for a job as a runner for a TV company and I wrote them a letter. I also sent them my (3) _____ with details of my education and other work experience. In my letter I said that I had always wanted a (4) _____ in TV and was happy to start at the bottom.

A: Were you nervous when you went for your (5) _____?

B: Yes, I was a bit. But they were very friendly and gave me a coffee.

A: What questions did they ask you?

B: They asked if I had a clean (6) _____ because I might have to do some driving. They also wanted to know about my computer (7) _____ and I told them I knew Word and Excel.

A: Did you need any other (8) _____ for the job?

B: No. But I think you have to be well (9) _____ for this kind of work, or you can't get everything done in time. And you also need a good (10) _____.

A: Really?

B: Yes. Because sometimes, if you didn't laugh, you'd cry!

A: Did they (11) _____ you the job straightaway?

B: No. They asked me for (12) _____. They wanted the name and address of my boss at my last company. And I also gave them the name of a woman I worked for in Italy.

A: Is it a (13) _____ job?

B: Yes. I work forty hours a week.

A: Do you make good money? Is it (14) _____?

B: No, but I don't mind. I'm not doing it for the money. My (15) _____ was really low but it went up after two months.

A: Is it a permanent job or is it (16) _____?

B: Well, I've got a twelve-month contract. They might renew it after that.

A: Do you find the work (17) _____?

B: No. It's hard work but the atmosphere is very relaxed. Anyway tell me about you. Are you still (18) _____?

A: No, I've got a job at last, but it's only (19) _____ – twenty hours a week. But they're sending me on a (20) _____ next week to improve my computer skills and after that they may offer me more hours.

- A *runner for a TV company* is someone who walks or runs from place to place carrying messages.

- The word *advertisement* is often abbreviated to *advert* or *ad*.

- The letters *CV* stand for the Latin phrase *curriculum vitae* which means literally *the racecourse of life*. In American English, a CV is usually called a *resumé*.

14 Verbs: communicating

Complete each sentence with a verb from the box in the correct form.

advertise	advise	congratulate	contact	demand	deny
explain	inform	insult	interrupt	persuade	present
remind	translate	warn	~~whisper~~		

1 'Ssh! Don't make a noise,' he __*whispered*__ . 'We don't want to wake the others up, do we?'

2 This is going to hurt a little,' the doctor _____ her.

3 'We regret to _____ you that flight BR 243 is delayed for three hours.'

4 I _____ to her three times how to use my mobile, but she still couldn't make a call.

5 I almost forgot to return the videos to the video shop. Luckily Claude _____ me.

6 I hate him. He called me a stupid idiot and _____ me in various other ways.

7 I know he copied his essay off the Internet, but he continues to _____ it.

8 She _____ me not to do the computer course but I'm still thinking of doing it because it might be useful.

9 At first I wanted to go to California on holiday but in the end we went to Maine because my sister _____ me it would be more fun. It was definitely the right choice.

10 Martha hasn't _____ me about the trip next week. I don't think she wants to come.

11 On Radio 6, they are _____ some very cheap flights to Florida at the moment.

12 Our first night in the hotel was terrible. The next morning we _____ to see the manager.

13 She didn't speak a word of Spanish so I had to _____ for her when we were in Madrid.

14 We were trying to have a conversation but her little boy kept _____ us.

15 While everyone was _____ the bride and groom after the wedding, we disappeared.

16 You look a bit like the guy who _____ the TV programme Lucky Day.

Don't forget the correct usage of the basic verbs: *say, speak, talk* and *tell*.
The verbs *say, speak, talk* can be used without an object:
He said that he was busy.
She spoke about her life in Africa.
They talked for hours.

These verbs can also be followed by *to* and an indirect object:
What did she say to you?
Who were you speaking / talking to?

The verb *tell* has to have an object:
I told him to leave.
She told him a lie / the truth / the answer / a story / the time.

15 Verbs: body and mind

Complete each sentence 1–16 with a verb from the box in the correct form.
Then match the sentences to the correct response a)–p).

> bleed   blow   ~~breathe~~   comfort   cure   dream   examine   faint
> hug   relax   rest   scratch   scream   sneeze   snore   weep

1   _Breathe_ in through your nose and out through your mouth.
    _j_

2   Don't _____ those mosquito bites. _____

3   What a fabulous cake! Can I _____ out the candles? _____

4   How can I stop my husband _____? He keeps me awake at
    night. _____

5   I _____ out loud when the bad guy jumped out of the
    cupboard. _____

6   I couldn't help _____ when my old cat died. _____

7   I'm about to _____. Atishoo! _____

8   I'm going to _____ your throat. Can you open your mouth?
    _____

9   Let's have a drink then go and _____ by the pool. _____

10 I've cut my finger. It's _____. _____

11 When she saw the blood, she _____ and fell on the floor.
    _____

12 That medicine has _____ my stomach ache. I feel fine now.
    _____

13 She saw him off at the airport and they _____ and kissed for
    five minutes. _____

14 We did our best to _____ her when she heard the bad news.
    _____

15 What did you _____ about last night? _____

16 You look tired. Why don't you go and _____ for an hour?
    _____

a	Bless you!
b	Yes, and you can make a wish.
c	Good idea. Don't you love holidays!
d	Great! But you'd better not eat any rich food for a couple of days.
e	How long was she unconscious?
f	I can't help it. They're terribly itchy.
g	I can't remember. But I woke up screaming.
h	I know how you feel. I cried when my dog died.
i	I'll put a plaster on it.
j	But my nose is blocked.
k	Make him sleep in another room!
l	OK. I feel very tired after that journey.
m	OK, Dr Fernandez.
n	So did I. It was so scary.
o	Was she really upset, then?
p	How long is he going away for?

At birthday parties in Britain (and many other countries), the tradition is that if you manage to blow out all the candles on your birthday cake, you can make a wish. Some of the other occasions on which you can make a wish, in British culture, are: when you catch a leaf that is falling from a tree; when you see the first evening star; when you see the new moon for the first time; when you pull the wishbone (breastbone) of a chicken or turkey with another person until it breaks, and you get the bigger bit.

16 Verbs: relationships

Complete the sentences with a verb from the box in the correct form.

> annoy apologize argue behave communicate criticize embarrass
> ~~fancy~~ force offend pretend regret separate share support

1 At first, I really _fancied_ him. I found him very attractive.

2 We started going out together and we _____ everything: money, clothes and even friends.

3 After a bit he began to _____ me with some of his habits. For example, he used to whistle all the time.

4 Sometimes he _____ me in front of my friends by drinking too much and telling the same stupid jokes over and over again.

5 Once he _____ me to go camping with his parents in Wales. I hate camping and I didn't get on with his parents.

6 We started to _____ about money. He said I was spending too much. I said he wasn't earning enough.

7 Once he came round with his mother and she _____ me by saying my flat was a mess.

8 I told her it was none of her business but David didn't _____ me against her.

9 I think we both _____ badly. He was lazy and passive and I was rude and aggressive.

10 I started to _____ him in front of people. I used to say he was mean with money, for example.

11   I always _____ afterwards, but he used to say, 'It's too late to say sorry.'

12   I hated spending any time on my own with him. I often went to the cinema in the evenings and _____ I was working late.

13   By the end of our relationship, we didn't _____ at all. We sat in silence all the time.

14   Eventually, we _____. I haven't seen him since 1998.

15   I don't _____ splitting up. We weren't happy together.

The phrase *to go out with someone* means to have a romantic relationship.
I used to go out with Jenny's brother when I was sixteen.
In American English, the word is *to date.*
We dated for about two years before we broke up.
Are Jim and Heidi dating? They're always together these days.

17 Word building: prefixes

A Make the opposites of these adjectives by putting the correct prefix in front of them. Choose from *un-*, *in-*, *im-*.

1	_un_ attractive	7	____healthy	13	____polite
2	____correct	8	____interesting	14	____popular
3	____dependent	9	____mature	15	____possible
4	____expensive	10	____moral	16	____practical
5	____fashionable	11	____patient	17	____sensitive
6	____formal	12	____pleasant	18	____usual

B Complete the sentences with one of the prefixed adjectives above.

1 She is so _____. She is seventeen but she acts like a six-year-old.

2 He's very _____. He doesn't get lonely although he lives on his own and takes all his holidays on his own.

3 The band's last CD was very _____. Hardly anybody bought it and they never played it on the radio.

4 The total is _____. They've charged us £15 for the fruit salad!

5 This sunny weather is very _____. It's normally cold and wet at this time of year.

6 Sally has been looking for a job for months. She looked miserable when Maria kept talking about her new job. Maria shouldn't be so _____. She should think about Sally's feelings.

7 We're having a very _____ party on Saturday evening. Come any time after nine and there's no need to dress up.

8 He can't even boil an egg or make coffee. In the kitchen he's a very _____ person.

9 Your diet is very _____. You eat too much fat and sugar and not enough fruit and vegetables.

10 She's always stealing from shops. In my opinion, she's completely
_____.

11 Mes Amis is an excellent restaurant. The food is delicious and it's
very _____. Even I can afford to eat there!

12 'I'm tired of waiting for this bus. Let's get a taxi.'

'Don't be so _____. The bus will be here in another five
minutes. We can't afford a taxi.'

- *un-* can go before any letters
- *im-* or *in-*? It's easy to decide. We only use *im-* before the letters *m*
  and *p*: *immobile, improbable*.

18 Around the house

Write the numbers 1 to 18 next to the correct words.

banister _11_   doormat _____   padlock _____

basket _____   extractor fan _____   plate rack _____

board _____   hat stand _____   rope _____

bucket _____   hook _____   string _____

candle _____   landing _____   strip light _____

CD rack _____   mop _____   thermometer _____

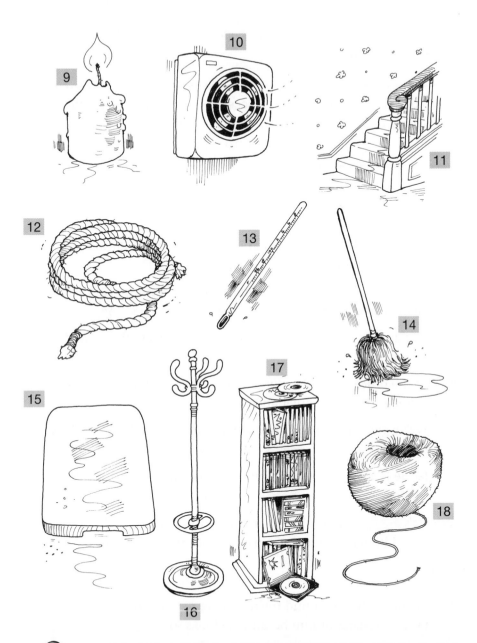

 The phrase *hat stand* seems slightly odd since in Britain, most people do not wear hats or hang them up. In fact, a hat stand is the thing we hang our coats on, which usually stands in the entrance hall of a house. In American English it is called, perhaps more sensibly, a *coat stand*.

19 Adjectives: people 2

The adjectives in the box below are all in the crossword. Read the clues and complete the crossword with them.

> adventurous   ambitious   eccentric   immature   moody
> nosy   obstinate   self-confident   strict   sympathetic
> talented   timid   violent

Across

1   They shouldn't get married at eighteen. They are far too _____ to take such an important decision.

5   Clive is having another exhibition of his paintings. He's also giving a concert next week. He is a very _____ person.

7   Tina is so _____. If I have a problem, she always listens and tries to help me.

8   At the office party, she stood in a corner and didn't speak to anyone. She's very quiet and _____

9   We've given her lots of good advice but she won't listen. She's very _____

11   Jackie is so _____. One minute she's laughing and the next she's sulking.

12   He's a _____ man. He was arguing with Tom last night and he ended up pushing him against the wall and shaking him.

Down

2   My uncle cycles around town in a big red hat and long red boots. Everyone stares at him because he looks so _____

3   She enjoys hot air ballooning and parachute jumping. She's very _____

4   He wasn't nervous about starting his new job. In fact he was very _____ and felt sure that he would do it well and enjoy it.

6 Michael already owns three restaurants but he intends to own a chain of them by the time he's thirty-five. He's very _____

7 Her parents are quite _____. She's seventeen but she has to be home by ten o'clock, even at weekends.

10 He's always asking me questions about my family and job. He's very _____

 Here's a way of increasing your word power. When you look up a new adjective in the dictionary, check if it has a noun form and write that down as well, for example *immature* (adj), *immaturity* (n).

20 Let's get technical

Complete the sentences with the correct words from the box.

> backup   CD ROM   crash   download   e-card   ~~file~~   ~~folder~~
> icon   key   keyboard   laptop   virus   website

1   'I can't find the letter I wrote to Judy anywhere on this computer.'

   'Wasn't it a ___*file*___ called Judy.doc? I think you saved it in the
   ___*folder*___ called Holidays.'

2   Apparently there's a terrible new computer _____ that can
   destroy all the information on your hard disk. The newspapers
   call it the Letter Bug.

3   I can't afford to buy new computer games so I _____ them
   from the Internet.

4   Computers are great but when they _____, you can lose a lot
   of your data.

5   I found a really interesting _____ yesterday with details of
   jobs and courses abroad. It's called www.jobshop.com.

6   If you want to open Internet Explorer, click on the _____.

7   It's too late to send Jasmine a birthday card to arrive by
   tomorrow. Let's send her an _____ instead.

8   I've just bought a _____ computer so I can write letters and
   articles while I'm on my round the world trip.

9   The _____ is the part of the computer that you type on.

10 To get a capital letter, press the shift _____ and the letter you
   want.

11 We have all our dictionaries and encyclopedias on _____.
   They take up less space than books.

12 You should always make a _____ of the work you do on the
   computer. Then if the computer crashes, you won't lose the work.

21 Toiletries, make-up and medicine

Write the numbers 1 to 14 next to the correct words.

aftershave __4__

antiseptic _____

aspirin _____

bandage _____

blusher _____

cotton wool _____

deodorant _____

hand cream _____

lipstick _____

mascara _____

plaster _____

shampoo _____

sponge bag _____

talcum powder _____

22 Verbs crossword

Read the clues and complete the crossword with them.

Across

1 Formal word for *leave*. (6)

6 I want to _____ a surprise party for Tim. Will you help me? (8)

8 The small patch of water on the ceiling is _____. Every day it's a bit bigger. (9)

12 Can you lend me a suitcase? I have to _____ for the weekend. (4)

13 I've passed all my exams. We're going to _____ tonight. (9)

14 There's no need to _____. We've got plenty of time. (4)

15 Yesterday we _____ across the lake in a little boat. (5)

16 Stones _____ if you drop them in water. (4)

17 You _____ the way and we'll follow. (4)

Down

1 I love _____ into water. It's more fun than jumping. (6)

2 She's better now. She has completely _____ from her illness. (9)

3 To get fit before you go climbing, you'll need to _____ (5)

4 I wouldn't _____ go parachuting. I'd be too scared. (4)

5 The bull _____ me from one side of the field to the other. (6)

7 He was _____ and beaten up by a gang outside the club. (8)

8 The police are _____ for a child who disappeared from his home yesterday. (9)

9 Wood _____ on water. (6)

10 Everyone watched the soldiers as they _____ through the streets. (7)

11 Formal word for *go in*. (5)

 The verb *search* is more common in written than in spoken English. It is
followed by *for* when it means *look for*.
They searched for the keys in every room of the house.
It is not followed by *for* when it means *to check a place or person*.
They searched the entire room but they couldn't find the keys.
The police searched the men but they didn't find any guns or drugs.

23 Animals

Write the numbers 1 to 18 next to the correct words. Then put the words in the correct group. There are two words for each group.

bat ___4___   leopard _____   swan _____

bee _____   lizard _____   tarantula _____

crocodile _____   mosquito _____   tortoise _____

frog _____   salmon _____   tuna _____

gazelle _____   scorpion _____   turkey _____

hedgehog _____   seal _____   whale _____

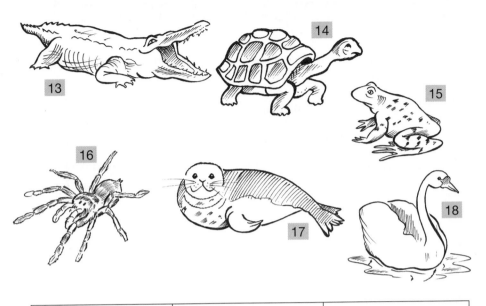

Large birds	African mammals	Fish
_____	_____	_____
_____	_____	_____
Small mammals	Sea mammals	Land reptiles
_____*bat*_____	_____	_____
_____	_____	_____
Insects	Poisonous animals	Animals that live in rivers (not fish)
_____	_____	_____
_____	_____	_____

- The first *o* in *leopard* is silent. It is not pronounced.
- **Question:** Where do you weigh a whale?
  Answer: At a whale-weigh station.

  The joke, in case you didn't understand it, is based on the fact that some English people, especially young children, pronounce *r* as *w*.

24 Compound nouns 1

A Find words in the box to complete the compound nouns. Write each compound noun.

1   <u>clothes</u> peg, <u>clothes</u> line

2   _____ varnish, _____ file

3   _____ hanger, _____ rack

4   _____ gown, _____ table

5   _____ number, _____ directory

6   _____ brush, _____ paste

7   _____ spray, _____ clip

8   _____ phones, _____ ache

9   _____ cream, _____ glasses

10 _____ polish, _____ lace

~~clothes~~
coat
dressing
hair
head
nail
shoe
sun
telephone
tooth

B Write the correct compound noun under each picture.

1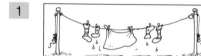

clothes line

2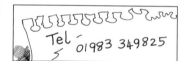

_____

3

_____

4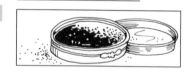

_____

5

clothes peg

6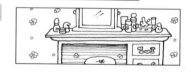

_____

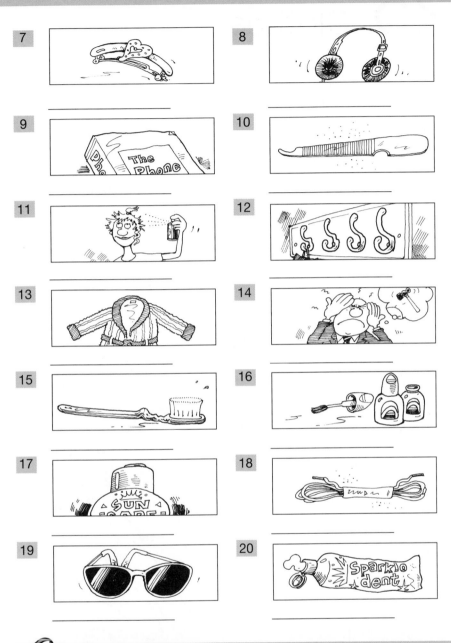

Test 28 on pages 50–51 gives further practice of compound nouns.

Some compound nouns are written as one word, some as two words and some have a hyphen (-) between the two nouns. Some words can be written in two ways. The forms *email* and *e-mail* are equally common. However, in modern English fewer compound nouns are being hyphenated. People write *ice cream* more commonly than *ice-cream*.

25 Clothes

Write the numbers 1 to 20 next to the correct words.

apron __4__   collar _____   hood _____   underwear _____

blouse _____   cuff _____   laces _____   uniform _____

bow tie _____   dungarees _____   pocket _____   vest _____

button _____   heels _____   sleeve _____   waistcoat _____

cardigan _____   hem _____   strap _____   zip _____

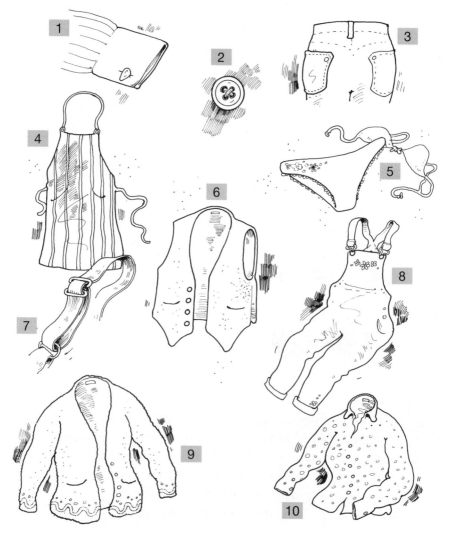

11

12

13

14

15

16

17

18

19

20

 • A *shirt* can be for men or women but a *blouse* is for women only.

• A *waistcoat* is called a *vest* in American English. In British English, a *vest* is an item of underwear.

26 Choose the word

Choose the word which best completes each sentence.

1   His work is getting worse and worse. Unless it ___*improves*___ , he'll fail his exams in the summer.

    a) gets well   b) improves
    c) increases   d) gets back

2   Oh dear! My watch has _____ !

    a) ended   b) stopped
    c) finished   d) completed

3   If you are paid to work for someone, then you are _____ .

    a) a slave   b) unemployed
    c) an employer   d) an employee

4   They didn't have a _____ of winning against Real Madrid.

    a) luck   b) wish
    c) time   d) chance

5   The _____ around this town is quite beautiful.

    a) countryside   b) scene
    c) nature   d) country

6   He's always telling me what to do. He's so _____ .

    a) cruel   b) bossy
    c) helpful   d) charming

7   Her parents gave her everything she asked for. She was really

    _____ .

    a) upset   b) ashamed
    c) full   d) spoilt

8 He's really lazy. He always _____ doing any of the housework.

a) gets away from   b) gets back from
c) gets over   d) gets out of

9 She wants to get to the top before she is thirty. She is very _____.

a) forward   b) ambitious
c) intelligent   d) advanced

10 John always arrives on time. He's so _____.

a) careful   b) boring
c) punctual   d) timeless

11 I was very _____ for all the advice she gave me.

a) glad   b) grateful
c) certain   d) pleased

12 They _____ all night to hear the results of the election.

a) stayed up   b) sat back
c) sat out   d) stayed down

- The word *grateful* is followed by the preposition *for* while *pleased* is followed by *with*.
  She was grateful for the money.
  He was pleased with his present.

- When *glad* means *grateful*, it is followed by *of*. When *glad* means *happy*, it is followed by *about*.
  She was glad of our help.
  I'm glad about their engagement.

- The word *certain* can be followed by *of* or *about*.
  Are you certain of / about this?

27 Cartoons 1

Match the words to the pictures. Write the letters a) to h) in the balloons.

a   Can I give you a hand?

b   Can you keep an eye on them for a minute?

c   Don't bother.

d   I wouldn't do that if I were you.

e   I'll do my best.

f   I'm afraid not. Can I take a message?

g   It wasn't my fault.

h   Sorry to keep you waiting.

 To give someone a hand and *to keep an eye on someone* are two examples of idioms that use parts of the body.

To *elbow* someone means to push past them.
They elbowed their way to the front of the queue.

If we can't stand something, we can say *I can't stomach it* or *I can't face it*.

Can you guess what the idiom means in this sentence?
I listened carefully in the history lesson but I couldn't concentrate.
The teacher's words went in one ear and out the other.

28 Compound nouns 2

A Find words in the box to complete the compound nouns. Write each compound noun.

1	business ___card___ , birthday ___card___	bag
2	drawing _____ , safety _____	basket
3	ear_____ , key _____	board
4	floor_____ , notice_____	~~card~~
5	laundry _____ , picnic _____	case
6	pen_____ , bread _____	knife
7	pillow_____ , brief_____	paper
8	plate _____ , roof _____	pin
9	sleeping _____ , hand_____	rack
10	wall_____ , news_____	ring

B Write the correct compound noun under each picture.

1

business card

2

_____

3

_____

4

birthday card

5
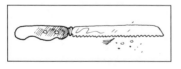
_____

6

_____

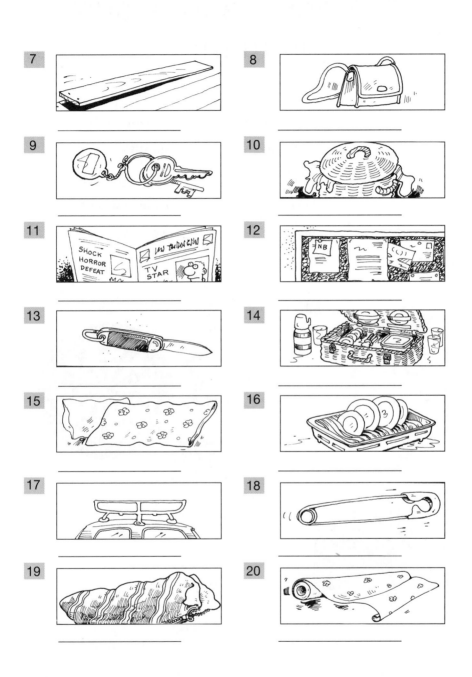

7

8

9

10

11

12

13

14

15

16

17

18

19

20

 When the first noun is an *–ing* verb form, the compound noun will be written as two words, for example *steering wheel, watering can, parking meter*.

29 Sports and leisure equipment

Write the numbers 1 to 16 next to the correct words.

binoculars __4__   fruit machine _____   playing cards _____

chess set _____   golf club _____   ski stick _____

dartboard _____   jukebox _____   snorkel _____

dice _____   knee pads _____   table tennis bat _____

fishing rod _____   net _____   weights _____

flippers _____

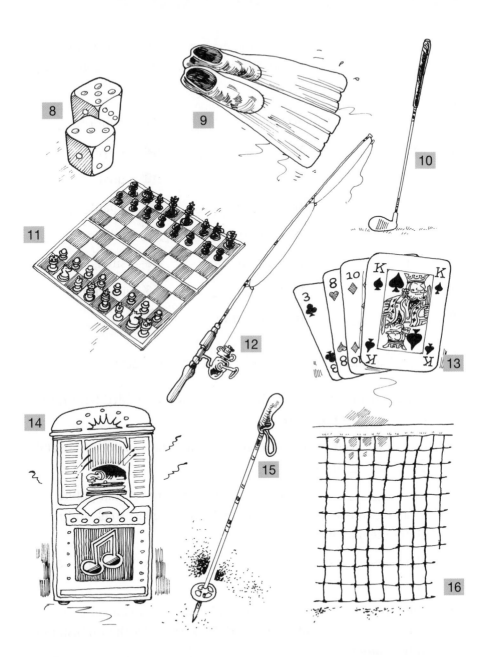

- Another word for *table tennis* is *ping pong*.
  Let's have a game of ping pong. Where are the ping pong balls?
- In American English a *fruit machine* is called a *slot machine*.

30 Abstract nouns

A Make abstract nouns by matching the first part of each word with the correct ending. Choose from the following: *-ment, -ance, -tion, -ence, -ship, -ity*.

1	achieve _ment_	9	experi_____	17	perform_____
2	agree_____	10	experi_____	18	possibil_____
3	appear_____	11	friend_____	19	qual_____
4	communica_____	12	import____	20	quant_____
5	confid_____	13	informa_____	21	relation_____
6	differ_____	14	inven_____	22	situa_____
7	dist_____	15	leader_____	23	unemploy_____
8	educa_____	16	opportun_____	24	viol_____

B Complete each sentence with one of the abstract nouns.

1 Congratulations! Cycling all the way around the Mediterranean is a fantastic _achievement_ .

2 Don't take your children to see that film. There's a lot of sex and _____ in it.

3 His _____ has increased since he went on that public speaking course. He gave a talk to 200 people last week and he didn't seem at all nervous.

4 I have a very good _____ with my boss. We get on very well.

5 There is a _____ that I will be out when you get here tomorrow. If I am out, you'll find the keys under the rubbish bin in the garden.

6   In Biology, we did an _____ to see the importance of light for growing plants.

7   She's always worried about her _____. She keeps changing her hair colour and going on diets to lose weight.

8   She's been a teacher for fifteen years. She has a lot of _____ with children of all ages.

9   The two sides talked all day but they couldn't reach an _____.

10   I wanted to visit Josie in New York but I didn't get the _____. I had to go to meetings every day until late at night.

11   There is terrible _____ in this country. There are over two million people without jobs.

12   These shoes didn't cost much but they are really good _____. They're leather and they're handmade.

13   To start with, Martin was in charge. When he got ill, Jill took over the _____ of the group.

14   Which _____ of the twentieth century do you think has changed people's lives the most?

15   'What is the _____ from London to Edinburgh?' 'I think its about 350 kilometres, but I'm not sure.'

 There's a story that a student of English once spelt the word *fish* like this: *ghoti*. When asked why, she explained that the *gh* gave the sound *f* as in *rough*, the *o* gave the sound *i* as in *women*, and the *ti* gave the sound *sh* as in *station*! While it's true that English spelling is not easy, there are patterns that you can learn like the ending *–tion*, which is pronounced /ʃən/.

31 Verbs: world of work

Match each worker to one of the activities they do in their job. Choose a verb from box A and a noun phrase from box B.

		A	B
1	an editor _edits magazines_	adds up	an audience
2	an accountant _____	checks	cakes
3	a comedian _____	makes	essays
4	an actor _____	delivers	figures
5	a singer _____	~~edits~~	land
6	an art restorer _____	entertains	letters and parcels
7	a decorator _____	marks	~~magazines~~
8	a baker _____	measures	meals
9	a college lecturer _____	performs	old paintings
10	a doctor _____	puts up	passports and visas
11	an immigration officer _____	records	patients
12	a refuse collector _____	cleans	plays
13	a surveyor _____	serves	the rubbish
14	a waiter _____	takes away	songs
15	a courier _____	treats	wallpaper

The noun *refuse* is pronounced differently from the verb *refuse*.

réfuse, with the stress on the first syllable = rubbish

refúse, with the stress on the second syllable = say 'no' to something

32 Filling in forms

Complete the form with the correct words from the box.

> birth   capitals   code   ~~complete~~   forenames   ink   length
> nationality   occupation   permanent   purpose   sex   signature
> status   surname   telephone   temporary   title

PRESTON PARK STUDENT HEALTH CENTRE

Please (1) __*complete*__ this form in BLOCK (2) _____ in blue or black (3) _____ .

(4) _____ : Mongiovi

(5) _____ : Maria Liliana

Date of (6) _____ : 11.11.75

(7) _____ : Female / ~~Male~~

(8) _____ : ~~Mr / Mrs / Miss~~ / Ms / ~~Dr~~

Marital (9) _____ : ~~Single~~ / Married / ~~Divorced~~

(10) _____ : Italian

(11) _____ : journalist

(12) _____ of visit: To study English at the Preston Park Language Centre

(13) _____ address: via Rosalia, 35, 90143 Palermo, Italy

(14) _____ address: 15 College Court Road, Brighton, Sussex

Post (15) _____ : BN1 6UZ

(16) _____ : 01273 487459

(17) _____ of visit: 1 MONTH

(18) _____ : Maria L. Mongiovi   Date: 15th August 2001

Official forms often state that they should be completed in blue or black ink. This does not mean that we have to use a fountain pen with ink in it. It just means that we must not use a pencil.

33 Adjectives: things

A   Put the adjectives into the correct category in the table.

> ~~beige~~   bitter   boiling   cool   cream   furry   gigantic
> humid   juicy   massive   minute   navy   oval   rectangular
> ripe   rough   smooth   triangular

Colour	Shape	Size
beige	_____	_____
_____	_____	_____
_____	_____	_____
Describing food	**Describing weather**	**Texture**
_____	_____	_____
_____	_____	_____
_____	_____	_____

B   Complete the sentences with the correct adjectives from the table above.

1   Don't pick those apples. They aren't _____ yet.

2   I always shave my legs in the summer. I like them to be nice and _____ when I go to the beach.

3   The temperature isn't that high but it's very _____ today. You start sweating as soon as you go outside.

4   I'm not thirsty. I just ate a really _____ orange.

5   Dark blue doesn't suit me so I don't look very nice in my uniform, which is _____ and grey.

6   I can't read the print in that dictionary. It's _____.

7   I gave my niece a big brown _____ teddy bear for her birthday.

8 Cats have _____ faces with the ears and the chin as the three points.

9 It's _____ here in the summer. We spend all day relaxing in the pool.

10 Our dining room table isn't exactly round. It's more _____.

There is a rule for the order of adjectives when several are used together.

opinion	size	age	style	colour	origin	material	purpose	noun
horrible	little			white				dog
lovely	short		curly	blonde				hair
beautiful	long			black		silk	party	dress
nice		old			French		soup	bowls

I was bitten by a horrible little white dog.
Who's that girl with the lovely short curly blonde hair?
She was wearing a beautiful long black silk party dress.
Where did you get those nice old French soup bowls?

34 Disasters

Complete the extracts from newspaper articles with the correct words from the box. Put the verbs in the correct form.

> crash (verb)   disease   drought   drown (verb)   earthquake   ~~famine~~
> flood   hijack   hurricane   kidnap (verb)   lightning   volcano

1 Thousands of children are dying of hunger in Ethiopia. The Red Cross is distributing food in the worst areas of the _famine_ but ...

2 The area around Boulder, Colorado, has not seen rain for nine months. During the long _____, water supplies have been brought in by lorry ...

3 A 53-year-old policeman _____ in the River Thames at Hammersmith, West London, last night. The man, Robert Fox, dived in to rescue his granddaughter ...

4 A massive _____ shook Los Angeles yesterday, destroying hundreds of buildings and a road bridge. It measured 7.2 on the Richter Scale ...

5 A twenty-eight-year-old mother of two was in hospital last night after she was struck by _____. The woman has slight burns on her arm. 'I was taking the dogs for a walk in the park when the storm started ...'

6 The _____ of the International Airlines plane ended last night when the terrorists released all the passengers and gave themselves up to the police.

7 Doctors have no cure for the mystery _____ which is spreading across northern India. Symptoms are sore fingers and toes and a fever.

8 Scientists say that Mount Etna will erupt in the next few days. Thick smoke started to pour from the _____ this morning and ...

9 Residents of Lewes, in East Sussex, had to swim across the main street yesterday. The _____ caused by recent heavy rain is the worst for 150 years.

10 A coach full of schoolchildren _____ on the M4 motorway last night. The driver and two children were taken to hospital suffering from cuts.

11 The 12-year-old son of a wealthy businessman was _____ in New York last night. Mr Tony Brancusi, the child's father, told journalists he had received a letter asking for $2 million for the return of his son.

12 A _____ in the Caribbean island of Nevis has killed fourteen people and left thousands homeless. 'The wind blew the roof off my house,' one survivor said.

Motorways in Britain are called *M* (for motorway) and a number, for example *M1, M4, M25*.
We use the definite article to refer to a motorway.
We were driving up the M40 on our way to Birmingham, when our car broke down.

35 Parts of a car

Write the numbers 1 to 18 next to the correct words.

aerial _12_

bonnet _____

boot _____

bumper _____

engine _____

gear stick _____

hand brake _____

indicator _____

mirror _____

number plate _____

petrol cap _____

seatbelt _____

speedometer _____

steering wheel _____

tyre _____

wheel _____

windscreen _____

windscreen wipers _____

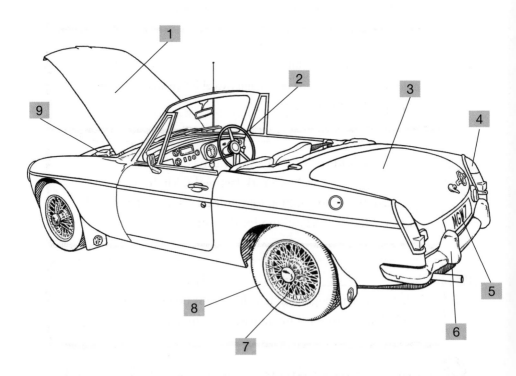

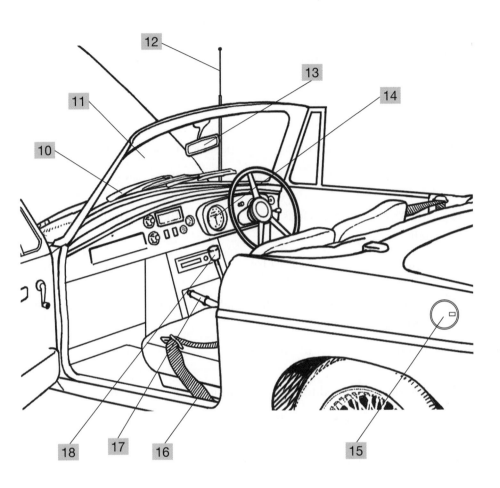

There are a number of differences in British and American English for the parts of a car. Here are some of them:

British English	American English
bonnet	hood
boot	trunk
number plate	license plate
bumper	fender

36 Prepositions 1

Complete the sentences with the missing words.

1 I'm very disappointed __*in*__ him. I thought he was a reliable person.

    a) on   (b) in   c) about

2 We had some difficulty _____ persuading her to come with us.

    a) in   b) for   c) to

3 She's very self-conscious _____ her height. She thinks she's too tall.

    a) after   b) for   c) about

4 I think we should divide all the leftover drinks and food from the party _____ ourselves.

    a) with   b) for   c) among

5 His ideas about education differ quite a lot _____ mine.

    a) to   b) from   c) with

6 Be careful! There are a lot of exceptions _____ this spelling rule.

    a) of   b) for   c) to

7 I think this song was inspired _____ an old Beatles one.

    a) by   b) of   c) from

8 This is entirely _____ you and me, but I think they're going to split up soon.

    a) among   b) between   c) for

9 Apparently Suzie's reading is _____ average. In fact, she's one of the brightest in her year.

    a) above   b) over   c) in front of

10 If we put the ladder _____ that wall, I'll be able to get on to the roof.

    a) under   b) beside   c) against

11 What are you holding _____ your back? Is it a present for me?

    a) behind   b) under   c) towards

12 We saw some horrible boys throwing stones _____ a poor old dog.

    a) for   b) against   c) at

Test 43 on pages 78–79 gives more practice of the use of prepositions.

37 Physical appearance

Write the numbers 1 to 17 next to the correct words.

bald _15_

beard _____

bun _____

chubby cheeks _____

double chin _____

earring _____

freckles _____

fringe _____

middle-parting _____

moustache _____

plait _____

pony tail _____

scar _____

side-parting _____

stubble _____

tattoo _____

wrinkles _____

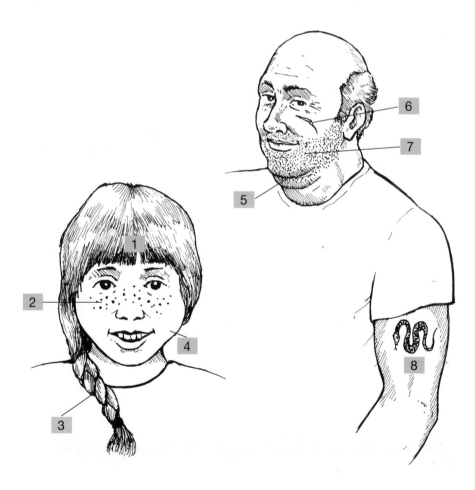

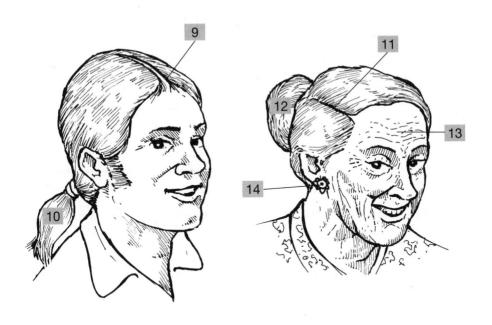

 In American English, a *plait* is called a *braid* and a *fringe* is *bangs*.
Who's the little girl with the braid and bangs?

38 Verbs: mostly in the mind

Complete the sentences below with the correct form of the words in the box.

admire	~~allow~~	compare	confuse	deserve	disapprove
intend	pretend	prove	recognize	solve	suppose
	tease	terrify	trust	wish	

1 You aren't __allowed__ to park here. Can't you see the sign?

2 She lent him the money because she _____ him to repay it. She didn't realize he was totally dishonest.

3 Don't tell the children ghost stories just before bed. You'll _____ them.

4 I _____ you'd give me some advice. Please tell me what to do.

5 I didn't want to go to the party so I _____ to have a headache.

6 I hadn't seen her for twenty years but I _____ her immediately.

7 I really _____ of people who always drive when they could walk. It's so bad for the environment.

8 I was _____ to finish this project last week but I don't think I'll finish it for another two weeks.

9 Money will _____ some of your problems but not all of them.

10 I want to _____ the prices of a few computers before I buy one.

11 People always _____ me and my sister because we are quite similar.

12 Adam is in love with Martina but he has never told her how much he _____ her.

13 Statistics _____ that women are better drivers than men. They have fewer accidents.

14 They _____ to leave at six in the morning but they didn't get going until eleven.

15 My friends always used to _____ me about my terrible voice. That's why I only sing in the bath now.

16 You've been working hard all week. I think you _____ a rest this weekend.

Librarian: No talking allowed in this library.
Schoolchildren: But we aren't talking aloud. We're whispering.

39 British and American English

How do Americans say these words? Choose from the words in the box.

American English					
apartment	cab	~~chips~~	clerk	deck	downtown
drugstore	elevator	faucet	parking lot		restroom
round trip	sidewalk	stand in line	subway		trash

1 Can you buy some **crisps** for the picnic?
(American English: _____*chips*_____)

2 Don't leave **rubbish** in the park. Take your empty drinks cans home with you.
(American English: _____)

3 Excuse me, where's the nearest **toilet**, please?
(American English: _____)

4 He works as a sales **assistant** in a big department store.
(American English: _____)

5 I can't walk any further. Let's take a **taxi**.
(American English: _____)

6 I have to go to the **chemist's** to buy some film for my camera.
(American English: _____)

7 I'd like a **return ticket** to Bristol, please.
(American English: _____)

8 It's quicker to go there by **underground** than by bus.
(American English: _____)

9 Take the **lift** to the fourteenth floor.
(American English: _____)

10 There's something wrong with the hot water **tap**. I can't turn it off.
(American English: _____)

11 We can leave the car in the **car park** behind the supermarket.
(American English: _____)

12 We could play a game of poker if someone has a **pack** of cards.
(American English: _____)

13 We had to **queue** for an hour to get tickets for the latest James Bond film.
(American English: _____)

14 You shouldn't cycle on the **pavement**. It's dangerous for the people who are walking.
(American English: _____)

15 She lives in a modern **flat** near the university.
(American English: _____)

16 I work in a bank **in the city centre**.
(American English: _____)

There are some possibilities for confusion when British and American people talk about food.

British English	American English
crisps	chips
chips	French fries

40 Cartoons 2

Match the words to the pictures. Write the letters a) to h) in the balloons.

a   Can you please sit still and stop biting your nails.

b   He's always been a bad loser.

c   I wish I hadn't already had lunch.

d   I'm sure we took a wrong turning somewhere.

e   Keep in touch.

f   Now what's all the fuss about?

g   Stand clear of the doors.

h   We're going clubbing.

 On the London Underground, just before the train doors shut, there is an announcement on loud speakers: *'Stand clear of the doors. This train is about to depart.'*

Very often, when the train arrives at a station, there is an announcement inside the train: *'Mind the gap.'* This is a warning for passengers getting off the train, about the gap between the train door and the edge of the platform.

41 Confusing words

Underline the correct word in each of the following sentences.

1   Was it Alexander Bell who (*invented* / *discovered*) the telephone?

2   The injured man was (*laying* / *lying*) on the road close to the crashed cars.

3   Amsterdam is a city full of (*channels* / *canals*).

4   Would you (*check* / *control*) these figures, Mr Brown, just to make sure they're correct?

5   The (*nature* / *countryside*) around this town is very flat and uninteresting.

6   Could I have a (*recipe* / *receipt*) for the things I've bought?

7   Oh, Jan, could you (*remember* / *remind*) me to phone the doctor this afternoon?

8   I wonder if you'd mind (*bringing* / *fetching*) John from next door? He's wanted on the phone.

9   What (*more* / *else*) did you do in Spain, apart from swimming and sunbathing?

10 Have you made (*an appointment* / *a meeting*) to see the bank manager yet?

11 I'll have to change this jacket. I bought it to go with my blue trousers, but it doesn't (*suit* / *match*) them after all.

12 I've got no money at all. I'm completely (*broken* / *broke*).

13 He really works hard. He's so (*industrious* / *industrial*).

14 Why don't you (*take* / *bring*) your girlfriend next time? We'd love to meet her.

15 She's very (*superstitious* / *supernatural*). She never walks under ladders and she doesn't dare go out of the house on Friday 13th.

One way of sorting out the correct use and meaning of pairs of words that you find confusing is to write pairs of sentences using each of the words. When you have finished this test, try writing sentences with each of the 'wrong' words. For example, sentence 1 above illustrates the use of *invented*. Here is a sentence showing the use of *discovered*:
Marie Curie discovered two new elements: radium and polonium.

42 Verbs: opposites

A   Match each verb on the left to its opposite in the box on the right.

1	accept	_refuse_
2	adore	_____
3	attack	_____
4	create	_____
5	encourage	_____
6	get worse	_____
7	increase	_____
8	obey	_____
9	praise	_____
10	vanish	_____

> appear
> criticize
> decrease
> defend
> destroy
> discourage
> disobey
> improve
> loathe
> ~~refuse~~

B   Complete the sentences with the correct form of the verbs above.

1   Everybody was against him at the meeting. Nobody tried to _____ him.

2   Her French has _____ a lot since she started having private lessons.

3   I absolutely _____ him and I'll never speak to him again. He's a cheat and a liar.

4   I got the part in the film thanks to Sandra. She's the one who _____ me to try for it.

5   I was following Jake through the forest when suddenly he _____ and I couldn't find him.

6   It's a fantastic book. All the reviews have _____ it.

7   We offered to lend him the money but he didn't _____ it.

8 She's got a really naughty puppy. It never _____ her when she tells it to sit.

9 The fire completely _____ the building. Only one wall was left standing.

10 The man jumped out of the bushes and _____ me with a knife. It was terrifying.

11 The rent on my flat has _____ by 20% this year so I won't be able to afford a holiday.

12 We always leave a light on in the house when we go out to _____ burglars from breaking in.

- The opposite of many verbs is formed with the prefix *dis-*, for example *obey / disobey, encourage / discourage, agree / disagree, prove / disprove, trust / distrust, approve / disapprove, appear / disappear.*
- The prefix *de-* sometimes means *to make less*, for example *decrease, devalue, depopulate, deforest.*

43 Prepositions 2

Complete the sentences with the missing words.

1   Those pills had a strange effect __on__ me. I won't take them again.

    a) for   b) by   c) on

2   I can't see any reason _____ this price rise.

    a) of   b) for   c) to

3   We noticed a huge bird _____ the distance.

    a) in   b) at   c) along

4   Children _____ twelve pay half price for entrance tickets.

    a) below   b) under   c) before

5   Please come away _____ the edge of the cliff. You're making me nervous.

    a) of   b) back   c) from

6   She's agreed to swap _____ me and do the Saturday shift.

    a) for   b) with   c) from

7   My grandfather died _____ a heart attack.

    a) by   b) with   c) of

8   How can I protect my plants _____ the snails?

    a) from   b) for   c) of

9   Have you seen that new advertisement _____ jeans?

   a) about   b) for   c) on

10   He won't admit _____ being a bad driver although he's had three
     crashes.

   a) for   b) about   c) to

11   She was given a reward _____ her courage during the rescue
     operation.

   a) for   b) about   c) of

12   We're trying to work out the cause _____ the fire.

   a) of   b) for   c) to

Prepositions are the hardest words to translate. How would you translate *on*
into your language in the following sentences? Can you use the same word
in your language for each of them?

There's a lot of traffic on the road today.

We met on the last day of the holidays.

They went on foot.

It had a strange effect on her.

That why it's best to learn new prepositions in a whole sentence. Don't try
to learn them as single words.

44 Types of transport

Write the numbers 1 to 18 next to the correct words.

ambulance __4__   ferry _____   scooter _____

bus _____   helicopter _____ sports car _____

canoe _____   lorry _____   submarine _____

caravan _____   motorbike _____   tractor _____

coach _____   plane _____   van _____

estate car _____   rocket _____   yacht _____

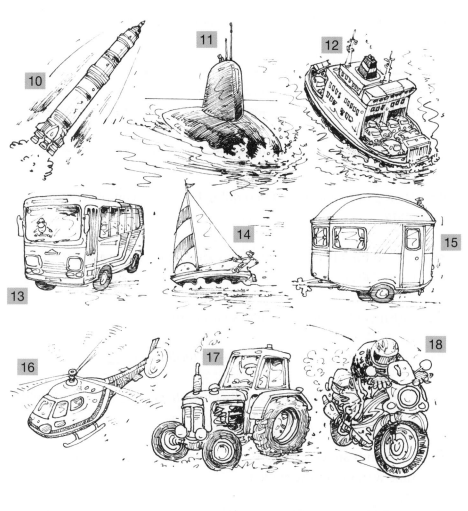

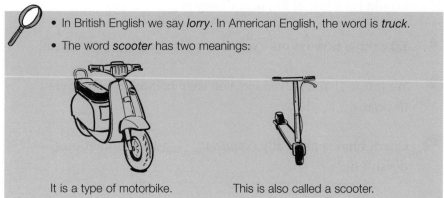

- In British English we say *lorry*. In American English, the word is *truck*.
- The word *scooter* has two meanings:

It is a type of motorbike.   This is also called a scooter.

45 Adjectives: synonyms

In each sentence give a synonym for the words in brackets. Choose from the following:

> absurd   anxious   attractive   cheerful   coarse   confident
> immature   intentional   ~~mad~~   pathetic   relaxed   reliable
> revolting   starving   weird

1 There's only one way of describing her. She is completely (*crazy*)
mad .

2 A good friend is someone who is kind, considerate and totally
(*dependable*) _____.

3 I wish you'd grow up! You're so (*childish*) _____.

4 I didn't mean to break it – it wasn't (*deliberate*) _____.

5 The food at the hotel was really (*disgusting*) _____. No one could
eat it.

6 Her hands are very (*rough*) _____ because she spends most of her
time working in the garden.

7 I could eat a horse! I'm (*really hungry*) _____.

8 Take those trousers off – you look (*ridiculous*) _____ in them!

9 We lost 6–1! You played like you were half-asleep! You were
(*hopeless*) _____!

10 Charles has some really (*strange*) _____ ideas sometimes,
doesn't he?

11 He's really (*good-looking*) _____. All the girls fancy him.

12 She's always (*worried*) _____ about something even when things are going well.

13 It's fun to be with him because he's so (*light hearted*) _____. With him, life always seems easy.

14 He's always totally (*calm*) _____. I don't think he knows the meaning of the word stress.

15 Try to be more (*sure of yourself*) _____ when you get on the horse. It will know if you are feeling nervous.

Usually words don't have identical uses even if their meanings are very similar. One word may be more formal than the other, or there may be a shade of difference in meaning. For example, *crazy, mad, insane*, all have the same meaning. However, *crazy* is more informal than the other two words. *Insane* is the most formal of the three. The words *crazy* and *mad* can both be used to mean *angry*.

46 Phrasal verbs 2

Complete each sentence with a phrasal verb in the correct tense. Sometimes you will have to separate the verb from the particle.

break up	call off	drop out	get by	get out of	go off
go on	hold up	~~put up~~	take up	turn down	work out

1   Diane phoned and asked if we could _put_ her _up_ for the night. (*give her a bed*)

2   Ed and Liz have _____. Liz is going out with Colin now. (*separated*)

3   He says he's sick of photography and he's going to _____ painting now instead. (*start*)

4   He was doing a degree at Harvard but he _____ after failing one of his exams. (*gave up and left*)

5   I didn't want to go to dinner with them but there was no way I could _____ it. (*find an excuse not to go to*)

6   I'm not very good at Spanish but I _____ when I was in Chile last year. (*managed to communicate*)

7   Marina was offered an amazing job in New York but she _____ it _____ because she wanted to stay in Boston. (*didn't accept*)

8   Our flight was _____ for three hours by bad weather. (*delayed*)

9   She _____ asking me questions until in the end I had to tell her the truth. (*didn't stop*)

10   She used to love scuba diving but she _____ it after her boyfriend got attacked by a shark. (*lost her enthusiasm for*)

11   The hotel staff had lost our booking and we had to stay somewhere else. But in the end everything _____ and we had a great time. (*came right*)

12   They've decided to _____ the barbecue because the weather is so bad. (*cancel*)

With many phrasal verbs, when the direct object is a noun, the noun can go before or after the particle: *We're putting up some friends for the night*, OR *We're putting some friends up for the night*. If the direct object of these phrasal verbs is a pronoun, the pronoun has to go before the particle: *We're putting them up for the night*. NOT ~~We're putting up them for the night~~.

47 Things to read

Complete the sentences with the correct words from the box.

album   atlas   brochure   calendar   catalogue   comic   diary
dictionary   directory   encyclopedia   index   manual   map
newspaper   recipe book   register   romantic novel   timetable

1   You read a **_newspaper_** to find out what has happened recently
in your own country and in the rest of the world.

2   In a _____ you find a list of things for sale, usually with
photos, plus their prices.

3   An _____ shows you where towns, rivers and mountains
are in all the countries of the world.

4   A _____ is a love story.

5   An _____ is a book, or a set of books, with information on
many different subjects in alphabetical order.

6   You can keep a collection of photographs or autographs in an
_____.

7   You look at a _____ to know the date and the month.

8   You can use a _____ to write down important dates of
meetings, for example. You can also use one to keep a record of
what happens in your life.

9   An _____ is an alphabetical list of names or subjects at the
back of a book. It gives the pages where you can find each of
these names or subjects.

10   If you have a _____ then you shouldn't get lost.

11   When something goes wrong with your computer, you can always try to fix it yourself with the help of the _____.

12   If you want to find out the times of trains or buses, you should look at a _____.

13   A lot of people choose where to go for a holiday by looking at the pictures in a tourist _____.

14   If you want to find out how to make a particular dish, you can look in a _____.

15   If you don't know a person's telephone number, you can look it up in the telephone _____.

16   You look up words in a _____ to find out their meaning.

17   A _____ is a magazine with picture stories. Speech balloons from the people in the pictures show what the people are saying or thinking.

18   A teacher uses a _____ to record how often each student comes to a class.

Sometimes it's easier to learn new words working with a friend. After you've done this test once, write the eighteen new words on small pieces of paper. Take turns picking a piece of paper and using the word on it in a sentence.

48 Classifications

Complete each group of words below with a word from the box. Then write the name for each group in the grid on page 89.

bear	boots	burglary	brochure	carton	darts
deodorant	earrings	flood	from	jazz	knickers
mascara	ostrich	~~plastic~~	sardine	silk	van	well	wet

1 wood, metal, glass, _plastic_

2 slowly, better, softly, _____

3 necklace, chain, bracelet, _____

4 near, behind, under, _____

5 mugging, shoplifting, drug-dealing, _____

6 rap, classical, folk, _____

7 chess, cards, pool, _____

8 cotton, nylon, wool, _____

9 raw, sticky, disgusting, _____

10 salmon, tuna, shark, _____

11 penguin, parrot, pigeon, _____

12 seal, whale, bat, _____

13 bra, pants, vest, _____

14 tin, tub, box, _____

15 shampoo, soap, bubble bath, _____

16 blusher, lipstick, powder, _____

17 sandals, slippers, shoes, _____

18 manual, catalogue, atlas, _____

19 coach, lorry, scooter, _____

20 earthquake, hurricane, drought, _____

#	1	2	3	4	5	6	7	8	9	10	11
1	M	A	T	E	R	I	A	L	S	■	■
2			V					■	■	■	■
3			W					Y	■	■	■
4		R		P					O		
5		R				■	■	■	■	■	■
6			S		■	■	■	■	■	■	■
7	G				■	■	■	■	■	■	■
8		L		T	■	■	■	■	■	■	■
9			J			T					■
10		I			■	■	■	■	■	■	■
11			R		■	■	■	■	■	■	■
12			M	M		■	■	■	■	■	■
13			D		R				■	■	■
14	C			T					R		■
15		O		L		T		■	■	■	■
16			K		■	■	■	■	■	■	■
17	F				W			■	■	■	■
18	P		B			C					
19			H		C		■	■	■	■	■
20		I				T			■	■	■

People usually find it easier to learn new words in a *set*. Try adding one more word to each of the sets on this page.

49 Homophones

Homophones are words that sound the same but are spelt differently. What are the missing homophones in these pairs of sentences?

1 I'm going on a diet. I've put on a lot of __weight__ .

Please __wait__ a minute. I won't be long.

2 I put on the _____ and the car stopped just in time.

This kind of china _____ very easily. Be careful.

3 Would you like another _____ of cake with your tea?

Everyone wanted the war to end and _____ to begin.

4 Can you untie the _____ in this string?

I'm _____ very good at science. I'm better at languages.

5 I didn't tell her what was in the parcel. She _____ by feeling it.

She was a _____ at a wedding I went to recently.

6 'Anyone who _____ gum in class will be sent out.'

I don't know what to _____ on this menu. There are so many good things.

7 You aren't _____ to smoke anywhere in this building.

Sorry, I wasn't talking to anyone in particular. I was just thinking _____.

8 Are you _____ you want to go out in this horrible weather?

Yes, I'd like to go to the beach and walk along the sea _____.

9 That man always _____ at me when I go past his shop. I don't like it.

Don't let's take the lift. I want to walk up the _____.

10   I've never jumped _____ than that. It's my personal record.

Where can I _____ ski boots? I don't have any of my own.

11   There were only ten _____ of seats in the hall so quite a lot of people had to stand.

He gave me a single red _____ on Valentine's Day.

12   Don't park there. It's illegal and you might get _____.

Where is my wallet? I can't _____ it anywhere.

13   Get me a needle and I'll _____ this button on for you.

She didn't pay me back the money last time _____ I refused to lend her any next time she asked.

14   I've had this teddy _____ since I was three.

We haven't yet bought any carpets for our flat. We've got _____ floorboards.

15   They've _____ the thieves who broke into our car.

I've got to go to _____ in three weeks to be a witness.

 Lots of silly jokes in English are based on words that sound the same but are spelt differently and have different meanings. Here's one of them:
Question: Why are people who work in a fish shop mean?
Answer: Their job makes them sell fish. *(selfish)*

50 Verbs: synonyms

A Match each verb on the left to the one on the right that is closest to it in meaning.

1	arrange	_organize_	cheat
2	bend	_____	contain
3	lower	_____	curve
4	exchange	_____	manage
5	include	_____	~~organize~~
6	lie	_____	realize
7	notice	_____	reduce
8	save	_____	rescue
9	spoil	_____	ruin
10	succeed	_____	swap

B Complete the sentences with the correct forms of the verbs above. If both verbs in a pair can go in the sentence, write them both.

1 Be careful! Very soon the road __*bends/curves*__ round to the right.

2 _____ down and touch your toes.

3 Have you _____ anything different about her? She's wearing contact lenses instead of glasses.

4 I am going to _____ a leaving party for them before they move to Australia.

5 He never tells the truth. In fact, he _____ all the time.

6 I'm going to take these shoes back to the shop and _____ them for a navy pair.

7 I'm not playing with him again. He always _____ by looking at other people's cards.

8 I've spent three hours trying to fix the car and all I've
_____ in doing is getting my hands dirty.

9 She's a hero. My son was drowning and she dived in and
_____ him.

10 This bill does not _____ service.

11 The government is going to _____ the amount of tax on
fuel next year.

12 This box _____ nothing but old letters and photos.

13 We didn't _____ to do much sightseeing because it was
so hot and humid all the time.

14 We had terrible rain and wind the whole time, and it
_____ our holiday.

15 When we got to the airport, she suddenly _____ she'd
left her passport at home.

Even when verbs have very similar meanings, they can't always be used in
the same way. For example, we can say *The road bends to the right.* OR
The road curves to the right. But we can't say ~~Curve down and touch your toes~~. We have to say *Bend down and touch your toes.*

51 Adverbs 1

Complete each sentence with the correct word from the box. Use each word once only.

> angrily   carefully   continuously   ~~easily~~   extremely   finally
> heavily   lately   luckily   patiently   seriously   well

1 They say it's difficult to get a job in TV, but I found one __easily__.

2 You'd better take an umbrella with you. It's raining _____ at the moment.

3 It's been a really hard day today, so I should sleep _____ tonight.

4 They lived very close to the motorway, and cars and lorries _____ passed their house during the night. It was really hard to sleep sometimes.

5 'Mind your own business!' he shouted _____.

6 _____ she had her mobile with her, so when she got lost in the forest, she was able to phone for help.

7 The weather has been _____ cold recently. In fact, this is the coldest November for over seventy-five years.

8 Have you got any idea what's happened to Annie? I haven't seen her _____.

9 He took his driving test for the seventh time and _____ managed to pass it.

10 The roads are very icy tonight, so drive _____.

11 He crashed his motorbike, but he wasn't going fast so he wasn't _____ hurt. He just cut his hand.

12 The crowd waited _____ for the movie stars to arrive.

 Test 58 on page 105 also practises adverbs.

52 Anagrams

An anagram has the same letters as another word, but in a different order.
Sort out these anagrams.

1. Change **tied** into something you do to lose weight. _____diet_____

2. Change **small** into big shopping centres. _____

3. Change **each** into a word that means *pain*. _____

4. Change **fade** into a word that means you can't hear. _____

5. Change **rested** into a very hot, dry place. _____

6. Change **sport** into places where ships stop. _____

7. Change **grown** into the opposite of *right*. _____

8. Change **skis** into something you do with your lips. _____

9. Change **teach** into something dishonest people do. _____

10. Change **miles** into a sign of happiness. _____

11. Change **inch** into a part of the face. _____

12. Change **drawer** into a kind of prize. _____

13. Change **cars** into a mark from a deep cut that doesn't go away. _____

14. Change **dusty** into something students do. _____

15. Change **safer** into bad feelings. _____

16. Change **boredom** into a place where you sleep. _____

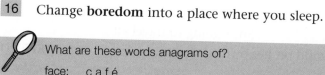

What are these words anagrams of?

face: c a f é

near: e _ r _

name: m _ _ n

notes: s _ o _ e

hated: d _ a _ h

thing: n _ _ _ t

When you have worked them out, make up clues like this: *Change 'face'
into a place for a coffee.* (Answer: *café*)

53 More word building

Use the words on the right to make a new word which fits the sentences.

1 At the show, the _magician_ kept pulling rabbits out of his hat.

MAGIC

2 Their dog barks a lot but he won't hurt you. He's completely _____.

HARM

3 There's no _____ between my old bike and my new one. The new one is ten times better.

COMPARE

4 I'm fed up with your _____. You're acting like a child.

BEHAVE

5 People are usually quite shy about discussing their _____ in public.

BELIEVE

6 This juice is full of artificial flavours. It tastes totally _____.

NATURAL

7 It's been a great _____ getting to know you. I hope we meet again soon.

PLEASANT

8 Put twenty pence in the machine and you can test your _____.

STRONG

9 She's very _____. She's going to travel all around the world on her own for a whole year.

DEPEND

10 There wasn't much of a _____ on the menu so I had a pizza again.

CHOOSE

11 _____ it rained all weekend so we couldn't go on the cycling trip we'd planned.

FORTUNE

12 I have very little _____ of the hotels and restaurants in this area. **KNOW**

13 We were all very impressed by the _____ of the countryside. **BEAUTIFUL**

14 In _____ to being good-looking and clever, he is also very rich. **ADD**

15 He's a very _____ person. He loses everything and is always late for meetings. **ORGANIZATION**

16 She grew up in the country and I think she had a very happy _____. **CHILD**

17 He's usually very kind and patient but just _____ he loses his temper. **OCCASION**

The suffix *-less* often has the meaning *without*. For example a *homeless* person is someone without a home.
The suffix *-ful* often gives the opposite meaning: *thoughtless* and *thoughtful* are opposites. Be careful, though. The opposite of *homeless* is not *homeful*!

54 Green issues

Complete the sentences with the correct words from the box.

> artificial   concrete   crops   ~~endangered~~   energy
> environment   factory   free range   fuel   organic   pesticides
> polluted   public transport   traffic   veal   wildlife

1 Rhinos are an __*endangered*__ species. We have to protect them or they will become extinct.

2 It's amazing how much _____ you can find in a city garden: foxes, hedgehogs, frogs and lots of birds and insects.

3 There's too much _____ in modern cities. Why can't we have more parks and open spaces instead of all these skyscrapers?

4 We need stricter laws to protect the _____ from the smoke and gases released by cars and factories.

5 I don't usually eat sweets. The _____ colourings and flavourings give me a headache.

6 This apple juice is _____. That means the fruit trees weren't sprayed with chemicals.

7 I only eat _____ chicken and eggs. I don't approve of chicken farms where the animals are kept in small cages.

8 Most farmers spray their _____ with _____ to stop insects eating them.

9 This farm is like a _____. The animals are treated like machines.

10 In order to produce _____, farmers take calves from their mothers when they are two weeks old and keep them in small, dark cages.

11 Oil is the main source of _____ in this country. It would be good to use cleaner sources like the wind and the sun.

12 There would be less _____ on the roads if the government made _____ cheaper.

13 Our new car is very economical on _____. It can do 100 kilometres on six litres.

14 A ship carrying oil crashed on the rocks here last year and now a lot of the coast is _____.

Try reinforcing your vocabulary in one area by making a word-web. For example, with words from this test you can make an environment word-web or a farm word-web. You could start your farm word-web like this:

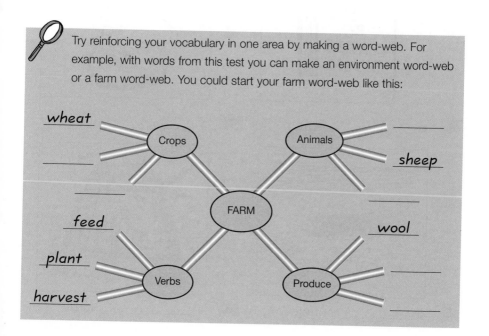

55 Adjectives and nouns

Choose the most suitable adjective for each noun.

damp	deep	haunted	painful	poisonous	stale	steep	sticky

stone ~~urgent~~ V-necked well-known

1 an ___urgent___ message

2 a _____ hill

3 a _____ writer

4 a _____ snake

5 a _____ hole

6 a _____ house

7   a _____ cut

8   _____ bread

9   a _____ cloth

10   a _____ sweater

11   _____ fingers

12   a _____ statue

Some adjectives go with particular nouns. The adjective *stale*, for example, usually goes with the noun *bread*. It can also go with *cake, biscuits, buns* and other baked food. We can't say that meat or milk is stale. Meat can be *off* or *rotten*. Milk can be *off* or *sour*.

I had to throw the sausages away. They were off. / They were rotten.

Don't use that milk. I think it's off.

56 Same word, different meaning

In each pair of sentences below, the missing word is the same but the meaning is different. What are the missing words?

1 _change_   Let's go out tonight for a ____. I'm fed up with cooking.
Have you got any ____? I've only got a £10 note.

2 _____ My brother can't stand the sight of blood. It always makes him ____.
Her voice on the phone was so ____ that I could hardly hear it.

3 _____ She doesn't have a ____ account. She keeps her money under the mattress.
We saw him sitting on the river ____ fishing.

4 _____ I can't ____ that man. He really gets on my nerves.
We saw a ____ in the forest when we were camping in California.

5 _____ You have to ____ three egg whites to make this pudding.
Argentina ____ Germany 2–0 in the final.

6 _____ I don't have to wear a ____ to work. I just go in jeans and a T-shirt.
She bent down to ____ up her shoelace.

7 _____ She had a cold and the ____ of her nose was red.
The waiter was really helpful so we gave him a big ____.

8 _____ She wants curtains that will ____ her carpet.
It was the most exciting football ____ I've ever seen.

| 9 | _____ | Use a first-class ____ if you want the letter to arrive by tomorrow. |
| | | Everyone began to ____ their feet in time to the music. |

| 10 | _____ | I'm tired. I think I'll go and ____ down for a while. |
| | | I didn't say that! That's a ____! |

| 11 | _____ | I need to go to the gym every day to try to get into ____ again. |
| | | A rugby ball is a different ____ from a football. |

| 12 | _____ | She dropped my favourite china vase and it ____. |
| | | I've just spent all my money on a new sound system. I am now completely ____. |

| 13 | _____ | I parked my car on a double yellow line and I got a £30 ____. |
| | | I heard the weather forecast and apparently it's going to be ____ today. |

| 14 | _____ | One, three, five and seven are odd numbers. Two, four, six and eight are ____. |
| | | I'm not going out ____ if it stops raining. I'm too cold and tired. |

| 15 | _____ | I have absolutely no ____ in politics. I like art, music and literature. |
| | | You can get about 6% ____ in this savings account. |

| 16 | _____ | She's a good teacher because she's very ____. |
| | | Doctor Fernandez has received another card from a grateful ____. |

Here are some silly jokes based on words that have two meanings.

A: Have you noticed any change in me?

B: No. Why?

A: Well I've just swallowed twenty-five pence by accident.

Question: How do you keep cool at a football match?

Answer: Stand next to a fan.

57 Rhyming words

Complete the sentences. The missing words rhyme with the words in brackets.

1 There's no-one on the tennis __court__. Let's go and play. (*port*)

2 My _____ is so sore I can hardly swallow. (*goat*)

3 Don't _____ your brother about his spots. He doesn't like it. (*please*)

4 We can't eat this bread, it's _____. (*rail*)

5 The air was so dusty it made me _____. (*trees*)

6 The rules at this school are very _____. You have to obey them. (*picked*)

7 The _____ of my shirt is filthy. I must go and change. (*dollar*)

8 It's getting very late. I _____ if they'll come now. (*shout*)

9 I don't wear much make-up – just lipstick and _____. (*louder*)

10 I'm going to water the garden. Can you turn the _____ on, please? (*toes*)

11 He's got a job as a _____ in a new French restaurant. (*deaf*)

12 Don't touch the cat. He's in a bad mood and might _____ you. (*match*)

13 She's a very _____ girl. She's got strange ideas about everything. (*beard*)

14 Alice fell off her bike last week and broke her _____. (*missed*)

15 Let's go into the garden and sunbathe on the _____. (*born*)

16 We need some _____ to tie around this broken suitcase. (*soap*)

17 You'd better not speak to me today. I'm in a really bad _____. (*rude*)

18 My brother has a _____ and he spends the whole summer sailing. (*shot*)

19 This house is haunted! There's a _____ in the attic. (*roast*)

20 Can you _____ some cheese to put on top of the pasta? (*weight*)

58 Adverbs 2

Complete the sentences with the correct words from the box. Use each word once only.

---

absolutely annually anxiously comfortably completely deliberately
fortunately ~~happily~~ hardly normally unexpectedly violently

---

1   Mike and Cathy Chambers have been _happily_ married for eighteen years.

2   It wasn't an accident! She did it _____! I saw her.

3   I _____ have toast and tea for breakfast but today for a change I had a boiled egg.

4   Have you seen Poppy and Dave's new house? It's _____ enormous!

5   My grandfather was sitting so _____ in the new armchair that he fell asleep.

6   When he returned to his village after fifteen years, he found that everything had _____ changed. The place wasn't a village any more – it was now a town.

7   His friends had changed so much that he _____ recognized them any more.

8   My parents arrived at my flat _____. I had no idea they were coming today.

9   There was an accident on the motorway this morning, but _____ no-one was hurt.

10   She waited _____ by the phone for news of her missing daughter.

11   I could tell he was angry because he banged his glass down on the table _____.

12   That book is published _____ but we haven't got this year's edition of it. We've only got last year's.

We form adverbs of manner by adding -*ly* or -*ily* to the adjective: *careful / carefully, angry / angrily*. When an adjective ends in -*le*, we form the adverb by deleting the -*e* and adding –*y*: *simple / simply*.

59 Choose the adjective

Complete the sentences on the left with the correct ending from the right.

1	A blonde girl or boy has __*fair hair*__.	very curious
2	An awkward person is _____.	offices in many countries
3	A contented person is _____.	clumsy
4	An ancient monument is _____.	about to fall down
5	An extraordinary experience is _____.	real
6	A nosy person is _____.	good at making things
7	A delicious meal is _____.	~~fair hair~~
8	A complicated story is _____.	debt
9	An imaginary illness isn't _____.	unmarried
10	A historical novel is _____.	fashionable and smart
11	An evil dictator is _____.	very tasty
12	A multinational company has _____.	about the past
13	A painful decision is _____.	meat
14	A secure shelf isn't _____.	a lot of money
15	A single person is _____.	amazing and unusual
16	A creative person is _____.	very old
17	A stylish girl is _____.	wicked and cruel
18	A successful business makes _____.	hard to make
19	A vegetarian meal doesn't contain _____.	satisfied
20	An unpaid bill is a _____.	hard to follow

 Some adjectives can only go with certain nouns. We can only use the word *blonde*, for example, to talk about people. We can't use it to describe the colour of an animal or a thing.

60 What's the verb?

Complete the sentences with the correct words from the box. Use each word once only.

break	catch	change	cross	deliver	~~grow~~	lose
make	open	roll	run	share	tell	tie	twist	win

1 Roses, plants, your hair are things you __grow__.

2 Letters, babies, parcels are things you _____.

3 Trains, buses, a cold are things you _____.

4 Doors, windows, a bank account are things you _____.

5 Shoelaces, knots, ribbons are things you _____.

6 Money, your mind, jobs are things you _____.

7 A border, a road, your fingers are things you _____.

8 A promise, a bone, a record are things you _____.

9 Lies, stories, jokes are things you _____.

10 A company, a race, a bath are things you _____.

11 Your job, your memory, weight are things you _____.

12 Competitions, prizes, battles are things you _____.

13 A bed, a decision, a mess are things you _____.

14 Your ankle, your knee, somebody's words are things you _____.

15 Dice, your eyes, cigarettes are things you _____.

16 An opinion, a room, a taxi are things you _____.

- A bilingual dictionary can be very useful for a quick translation of simple words. However, you must be careful to find the right translation if a word has several meanings. For example, in English we can use the verb *catch* in both these sentences: *I'm in a hurry, I have to catch a train*. and *Keep warm or you'll catch a cold*. Can you use the same word in your language?

- If somebody decides they want to have long hair, they say they are growing it.

  'Your hair's longer than usual.'

  'Yes, I'm growing it. I haven't had it cut for six months now.'

Answers

Test 1
blender 4
bottle opener 9
briefcase 6
broom 3
coat hanger 12
dustpan 2
light bulb 1
pepper grinder 10
potato peeler 7
suitcase 5
tea towel 8
tray 11

Test 2
Across
1 superficial
6 relaxed
8 popular
10 reliable
13 brave
14 honest
15 patient
17 grateful

Down
1 sensible
2 independent
3 lively
4 miserable
5 mature
7 jealous
9 weird
11 generous
12 proud
16 warm

Test 3
1 got over
2 told him off
3 ran out of
4 brought them up
5 put it off
6 picking me up
7 shows off
8 broke down
9 took off
10 put out

11 kept on
12 blew it up
13 knocked him out
14 turned up
15 set out
16 cut down
17 let her down
18 hung up

Test 4
ankle 12
bottom 1
cheek 5
chest 10
chin 4
elbow 9
lips 6
stomach 11
throat 3
thumb 7
waist 2
wrist 8

Test 5
1 k potatoes
2 g eggs
3 b bread
4 h fish
5 a boiled eggs
6 f curry
7 d chocolate
8 m steak
9 c cola
10 i milk
11 e cream
12 j mineral water
13 l tea
14 o wine
15 n tomatoes

Test 6
branch 4
burglar alarm 12
bush 15
chimney 8
door handle 9
dustbin 3
flowerpot 2

French windows 6
greenhouse 5
hedge 16
hose 1
lawn 10
letterbox 7
patio 13
satellite dish 11
tap 14

Test 7
1 rational
2 tiny
3 artificial
4 exciting
5 cautious
6 broad-minded
7 sudden
8 uninterested
9 unlucky
10 sensitive
11 light-hearted
12 pessimistic
13 delicious
14 gentle

a emotional
b disgusting
c broad-minded
d aggressive
e artificial
f gradual
g optimistic
h daring
i pessimistic
j sensitive

Test 8
1 burglar
2 dealers
3 theft
4 hooligans
5 drink driving
6 speeding
7 bullies
8 fine
9 judge
10 shoplifting

11 violence
12 graffiti
13 gangs
14 robbers
15 mugged

Test 9
1 model
2 speech therapist
3 farmer
4 cashier
5 caretaker
6 driving instructor
7 pilot
8 astronaut
9 estate agent
10 chef
11 diver
12 lawyer
13 engineer
14 surgeon
15 lifeguard

Test 10
beat 6
chop 3
grate 5
heat 11
mix 4
peel 8
roast 1
slice 7
spread 10
squeeze 2
stir 12
whip 9

Test 11
1 b) put up
2 a) an only
3 c) left
4 c) get on
5 d) bring up
6 b) regret
7 b) support
8 c) bargain
9 a) save
10 d) unemployed
11 a) beat
12 b) platform

Test 12
aubergine 4
broccoli 1
cabbage 12
cauliflower 8
cherry 5
coconut 9
courgette 3
cucumber 2
fig 14
onion 11
peach 13
pepper 6
plum 10
tangerine 7

Test 13
1 application form
2 advertisement
3 CV
4 career
5 interview
6 driving licence
7 skills
8 qualifications
9 organized
10 sense of humour
11 offer
12 references
13 full-time
14 well-paid
15 starting salary
16 temporary
17 stressful
18 unemployed
19 part-time
20 training course

Test 14
1 whispered
2 warned
3 inform
4 explained
5 reminded
6 insulted
7 deny
8 advised
9 persuaded
10 contacted
11 advertising
12 demanded

13 translate
14 interrupting
15 congratulating
16 presents

Test 15
1 Breathe (j)
2 scratch (f)
3 blow (b)
4 snoring (k)
5 screamed (n)
6 weeping (h)
7 sneeze (a)
8 examine (m)
9 relax (c)
10 bleeding (i)
11 fainted (e)
12 cured (d)
13 hugged (p)
14 comfort (o)
15 dream (g)
16 rest (l)

Test 16
1 fancied
2 shared
3 annoy
4 embarrassed
5 forced
6 argue
7 offended
8 support
9 behaved
10 criticize
11 apologized
12 pretended
13 communicate
14 separated
15 regret

Test 17
A
1 unattractive
2 incorrect
3 independent
4 inexpensive
5 unfashionable
6 informal
7 unhealthy
8 uninteresting
9 immature
10 immoral

11 impatient
12 unpleasant
13 impolite
14 unpopular
15 impossible
16 impractical
17 insensitive
18 unusual

B
1 immature
2 independent
3 unpopular
4 incorrect
5 unusual
6 insensitive
7 informal
8 impractical
9 unhealthy
10 immoral
11 inexpensive
12 impatient

Test 18
banister 11
basket 4
board 15
bucket 2
candle 9
CD rack 17
doormat 1
extractor fan 10
hat stand 16
hook 3
landing 7
mop 14
padlock 5
plate rack 6
rope 12
string 18
strip light 8
thermometer 13

Test 19
Across
1 immature
5 talented
7 sympathetic
8 timid
9 obstinate
11 moody
12 violent

Down
2 eccentric
3 adventurous
4 self-confident
6 ambitious
7 strict
10 nosy

Test 20
1 file/folder
2 virus
3 download
4 crash
5 website
6 icon
7 e-card
8 laptop
9 keyboard
10 key
11 CD ROM
12 backup

Test 21
aftershave 4
antiseptic 14
aspirin 7
bandage 3
blusher 12
cotton wool 8
deodorant 1
hand cream 2
lipstick 10
mascara 13
plaster 5
shampoo 11
sponge bag 9
talcum powder 6

Test 22
Across
1 depart
6 organize
8 spreading
12 pack
13 celebrate
14 rush
15 rowed
16 sink
17 lead

Down
1 diving
2 recovered
3 train
4 dare
5 chased
7 attacked
8 searching
9 floats
10 marched
11 enter

Test 23
bat 4
bee 1
crocodile 13
frog 15
gazelle 5
hedgehog 9
leopard 7
lizard 12
mosquito 2
salmon 6
scorpion 11
seal 17
swan 18
tarantula 16
tortoise 14
tuna 8
turkey 3
whale 10

Large birds
swan, turkey

African mammals
gazelle, leopard

Fish
salmon, tuna

Small mammals
bat, hedgehog

Sea mammals
seal, whale

Land reptiles
lizard, tortoise

Insects
bee, mosquito

Poisonous animals
scorpion, tarantula

Animals that live in rivers (not fish)
crocodile, frog

Test 24
A
1 clothes
2 nail
3 coat
4 dressing
5 telephone
6 tooth
7 hair
8 head
9 sun
10 shoe

B
1 clothes line
2 telephone number
3 coat hanger
4 shoe polish
5 clothes peg
6 dressing table
7 hair clip
8 headphones
9 telephone directory
10 nail file
11 hair spray
12 coat rack
13 dressing gown
14 headache
15 toothbrush
16 nail varnish
17 sun cream
18 shoelace
19 sunglasses
20 toothpaste

Test 25
apron 4
blouse 10
bow tie 15
button 2
cardigan 9
collar 11
cuff 1
dungarees 8
heels 20
hem 16
hood 19
laces 14

pocket 3
sleeve 17
strap 7
underwear 5
uniform 12
vest 18
waistcoat 6
zip 13

Test 26
1 b) improves
2 b) stopped
3 d) an employee
4 d) chance
5 a) countryside
6 b) bossy
7 d) spoilt
8 d) gets out of
9 b) ambitious
10 c) punctual
11 b) grateful
12 a) stayed up

Test 27
1 h) Sorry to keep you waiting.
2 e) I'll do my best.
3 f) I'm afraid not. Can I take a message?
4 g) It wasn't my fault.
5 a) Can I give you a hand?
6 b) Can you keep an eye on them for a minute?
7 c) Don't bother.
8 d) I wouldn't do that if I were you.

Test 28
A
1 card
2 pin
3 ring
4 board
5 basket
6 knife
7 case
8 rack
9 bag
10 paper

B
1 business card
2 earring
3 drawing pin
4 birthday card
5 bread knife
6 briefcase
7 floorboard
8 handbag
9 key ring
10 laundry basket
11 newspaper
12 notice board
13 penknife
14 picnic basket
15 pillow case
16 plate rack
17 roof rack
18 safety pin
19 sleeping bag
20 wallpaper

Test 29
binoculars 4
chess set 11
dartboard 3
dice 8
fishing rod 12
flippers 9
fruit machine 2
golf club 10
jukebox 14
knee pads 1
net 16
playing cards 13
ski stick 15
snorkel 5
table tennis bat 7
weights 6

Test 30
A
1 achievement
2 agreement
3 appearance
4 communication
5 confidence
6 difference
7 distance
8 education
9 experience

10 experiment
11 friendship
12 importance
13 information
14 invention
15 leadership
16 opportunity
17 performance
18 possibility
19 quality
20 quantity
21 relationship
22 situation
23 unemployment
24 violence

B
1 achievement
2 violence
3 confidence
4 relationship
5 possibility
6 experiment
7 appearance
8 experience
9 agreement
10 opportunity
11 unemployment
12 quality
13 leadership
14 invention
15 distance

Test 31
1 edits magazines
2 adds up figures
3 entertains an audience
4 performs plays
5 records songs
6 cleans old paintings
7 puts up wallpaper
8 makes cakes
9 marks essays
10 treats patients
11 checks passports and visas
12 takes away the rubbish
13 measures land
14 serves meals

15 delivers letters and parcels

Test 32
1 complete
2 capitals
3 ink
4 surname
5 forenames
6 birth
7 sex
8 title
9 status
10 nationality
11 occupation
12 purpose
13 permanent
14 temporary
15 code
16 telephone
17 length
18 signature

Test 33
A
Colour
beige, cream, navy
Shape
rectangular, oval, triangular
Size
gigantic, massive, minute
Describing food
bitter, juicy, ripe
Describing weather
boiling, cool, humid
Texture
furry, rough, smooth

B
1 ripe
2 smooth
3 humid
4 juicy
5 navy
6 minute
7 furry
8 triangular
9 boiling
10 oval

Test 34
1 famine
2 drought
3 drowned
4 earthquake
5 lightning
6 hijack
7 disease
8 volcano
9 flood
10 crashed
11 kidnapped
12 hurricane

Test 35
aerial 12
bonnet 1
boot 3
bumper 6
engine 9
gear stick 18
hand brake 17
indicator 4
mirror 13
number plate 5
petrol cap 15
seatbelt 16
speedometer 14
steering wheel 2
tyre 8
wheel 7
windscreen 11
windscreen wipers 10

Test 36
1 b) in
2 a) in
3 c) about
4 c) among
5 b) from
6 c) to
7 a) by
8 b) between
9 a) above
10 c) against
11 a) behind
12 c) at

Test 37
bald 15
beard 17
bun 12
chubby cheeks 4
double chin 5
earring 14
freckles 2
fringe 1
middle-parting 9
moustache 16
plait 3
pony tail 10
scar 6
side-parting 11
stubble 7
tattoo 8
wrinkles 13

Test 38
1 allowed
2 trusted
3 terrify
4 wish
5 pretended
6 recognized
7 disapprove
8 supposed
9 solve
10 compare
11 confuse
12 admires
13 prove
14 intended
15 tease
16 deserve

Test 39
1 chips
2 trash
3 restroom
4 clerk
5 cab
6 drugstore
7 round trip
8 subway
9 elevator
10 faucet
11 parking lot
12 deck
13 stand in line
14 sidewalk
15 apartment
16 downtown

Test 40
1 h
2 g
3 b
4 d
5 a
6 f
7 e
8 c

Test 41
1 invented
2 lying
3 canals
4 check
5 countryside
6 receipt
7 remind
8 fetching
9 else
10 an appointment
11 match
12 broke
13 industrious
14 bring
15 superstitious

Test 42
A
1 refuse
2 loathe
3 defend
4 destroy
5 discourage
6 improve
7 decrease
8 disobey
9 criticize
10 appear

B
1 defend
2 improved
3 loathe
4 encouraged
5 vanished
6 praised
7 accept
8 obeys
9 destroyed
10 attacked
11 increased
12 discourage

Test 43
1 c) on
2 b) for
3 a) in
4 b) under
5 c) from
6 b) with
7 c) of
8 a) from
9 b) for
10 c) to
11 a) for
12 a) of

Test 44
ambulance 4
bus 9
canoe 6
caravan 15
coach 13
estate car 5
ferry 12
helicopter 16
lorry 7
motorbike 18
plane 3
rocket 10
scooter 1
sports car 8
submarine 11
tractor 17
van 2
yacht 14

Test 45
1 mad
2 reliable
3 immature
4 intentional
5 revolting
6 coarse
7 starving
8 absurd
9 pathetic
10 weird
11 attractive

12 anxious
13 cheerful
14 relaxed
15 confident

Test 46
1 put her up
2 broken up
3 take up
4 dropped out
5 get out of
6 got by
7 turned it down
8 held up
9 went on
10 went off
11 worked out
12 call off

Test 47
1 newspaper
2 catalogue
3 atlas
4 romantic novel
5 encyclopedia
6 album
7 calendar
8 diary
9 index
10 map
11 manual
12 timetable
13 brochure
14 recipe book
15 directory
16 dictionary
17 comic
18 register

Test 48
1 plastic/materials
2 well/adverbs
3 earrings/jewellery
4 from/prepositions
5 burglary/crimes
6 jazz/music
7 darts/games
8 silk/cloth
9 wet/adjectives
10 sardine/fish
11 ostrich/birds
12 bear/mammals

13 knickers/underwear
14 carton/containers
15 deodorant/toiletries
16 mascara/make-up
17 boots/footwear
18 brochure/publications
19 van/vehicles
20 flood/disasters

Test 49
1 weight, wait
2 brakes, breaks
3 piece, peace
4 knot, not
5 guessed, guest
6 chews, choose
7 allowed, aloud
8 sure, shore
9 stares, stairs
10 higher, hire
11 rows, rose
12 fined, find
13 sew, so
14 bear, bare
15 caught, court

Test 50
A
1 organize
2 curve
3 reduce
4 swap
5 contain
6 cheat
7 realize
8 rescue
9 ruin
10 manage

B
1 bends/curves
2 Bend
3 noticed
4 arrange/organize
5 lies
6 exchange/swap
7 cheats
8 succeeded
9 saved/rescued
10 include
11 lower/reduce
12 contains

13 manage
14 spoilt/ruined
15 noticed/realized

Test 51
1 easily
2 heavily
3 well
4 continuously
5 angrily
6 Luckily
7 extremely
8 lately
9 finally
10 carefully
11 seriously
12 patiently

Test 52
1 diet
2 malls
3 ache
4 deaf
5 desert
6 ports
7 wrong
8 kiss
9 cheat
10 smile
11 chin
12 reward
13 scar
14 study
15 fears
16 bedroom

Tip
café
earn
mean
stone
death
night

Test 53
1 magician
2 harmless
3 comparison
4 behaviour
5 beliefs
6 unnatural
7 pleasure

8 strength
9 independent
10 choice
11 Unfortunately
12 knowledge
13 beauty
14 addition
15 disorganized
16 childhood
17 occasionally

Test 54
1 endangered
2 wildlife
3 concrete
4 environment
5 artificial
6 organic
7 free range
8 crops, pesticides
9 factory
10 veal
11 energy
12 traffic, public transport
13 fuel
14 polluted

Test 55
1 urgent
2 steep
3 well-known
4 poisonous
5 deep
6 haunted
7 painful
8 stale
9 damp
10 V-necked
11 sticky
12 stone

Test 56
1 change
2 faint
3 bank
4 bear
5 beat

6 tie
7 tip
8 match
9 stamp
10 lie
11 shape
12 broke
13 fine
14 even
15 interest
16 patient

Test 57
1 court
2 throat
3 tease
4 stale
5 sneeze
6 strict
7 collar
8 doubt
9 powder
10 hose
11 chef
12 scratch
13 weird
14 wrist
15 lawn
16 rope
17 mood
18 yacht
19 ghost
20 grate

Test 58
1 happily
2 deliberately
3 normally
4 absolutely
5 comfortably
6 completely
7 hardly
8 unexpectedly
9 fortunately
10 anxiously
11 violently
12 annually

Test 59
1 fair hair
2 clumsy
3 satisfied
4 very old
5 amazing and unusual
6 very curious
7 very tasty
8 hard to follow
9 real
10 about the past
11 wicked and cruel
12 offices in many countries
13 hard to make
14 about to fall down
15 unmarried
16 good at making things
17 fashionable and smart
18 a lot of money
19 meat
20 debt

Test 60
1 grow
2 deliver
3 catch
4 open
5 tie
6 change
7 cross
8 break
9 tell
10 run
11 lose
12 win
13 make
14 twist
15 roll
16 share

Word list

The numbers after the entries are the tests in which they appear.

A
about 36
above 36
absolutely 58
absurd 45
accept 42
accountant 31
ache 52
achievement 30
actor 31
add up 31
addition 53
admire 38
adore 42
adventurous 19
advertise 14
advertisement 13
advise 14
aerial 35
aftershave 21
against 36
aggressive 7
agreement 30
album 47
allow 38
aloud 49
amazing 59
ambitious 19
ambulance 44
among 36
angrily 51
ankle 4
annoy 16
annually 58
antiseptic 21
anxious 45
anxiously 58
apartment 39
apologize 16
appear 42
appearance 30
application form 13
appointment 41
apron 25

argue 16
arrange 50
art restorer 31
artificial 7
aspirin 21
astronaut 9
at 36
atlas 47
attack 22
attractive 45
aubergine 12
audience 31

B
backup 20
baker 31
bald 37
bandage 21
banister 18
bank 56
bare 49
bargain 11
basket 18
bat 23
bear 48
beard 37
beat 10
beauty 53
bedroom 52
bee 23
behave 16
behaviour 53
behind 36
beige 33
beliefs 53
bend 50
between 36
binoculars 29
birth 32
birthday card 28
bitter 33
bleed 15
blender 1
blouse 25
blow 15

blow up 3
blusher 21
board 18
boiled eggs 5
boiling 33
bonnet 35
boot 35
boots 48
bossy 26
bottle opener 1
bottom 4
bow tie 25
brakes 49
brake light 35
branch 6
brave 2
bread 5
bread knife 28
break 49
break down 3
break up 46
breathe 15
briefcase 1
bring 41
bring up 3
broad-minded 7
broccoli 12
brochure 47
broke 41
broom 1
bucket 18
bullies 8
bumper 35
bun 37
burglar 8
burglar alarm 6
burglary 48
bus 44
bush 6
business card 28
button 25
by 36

C
cab 39

cabbage 12
cake 31
calendar 47
call off 46
canals 41
candle 18
canoe 44
capitals 32
caravan 44
cardigan 25
career 13
carefully 51
caretaker 9
carton 48
cashier 9
catalogue 47
catch 49
cauliflower 12
cautious 7
CD rack 18
CD ROM 20
celebrate 22
chance 26
change 56
chase 22
cheat 50
check 31
cheek 4
cheerful 45
chef 9
cherry 12
chess set 29
chest 4
chew 49
childhood 53
chimney 6
chin 4
chips 39
chocolate 5
choice 53
choose 49
chop 10
chubby cheeks 37
clean 31
clerk 39
clothes line 24
clothes peg 24
clumsy 59
coach 44
coarse 45

coat hanger 1
coat rack 24
coconut 12
code 32
cola 5
collar 25
college lecturer 31
comedian 31
comfort 15
comfortably 58
comic 47
communicate 16
communication 30
compare 38
comparison 53
complete 32
completely 58
concrete 54
confidence 30
confident 45
confuse 38
congratulate 14
contact 14
contain 50
continuously 51
cool 33
cotton wool 21
countries 59
countryside 26
courgette 12
courier 31
court 49
crash 20
cream 5
create 42
criticize 16
crocodile 23
crops 54
cross 60
cruel 59
cucumber 12
cuff 25
cure 15
curious 59
curry 5
curve 50
cut down 3
CV 13

D
damp 55
dare 22
daring 7
dartboard 29
darts 48
deaf 52
dealers 8
debt 59
deck 39
decorator 31
decrease 42
deep 55
defend 42
deliberately 58
delicious 7
deliver 31
demand 14
deny 14
deodorant 21
depart 22
desert 52
deserve 38
destroy 42
diary 47
dice 29
dictionary 47
diet 52
difference 30
directory 47
disapprove 38
discourage 42
disease 34
disgusting 7
disobey 42
disorganized 53
distance 30
diver 9
diving 22
doctor 31
door handle 6
doormat 18
double chin 37
doubt 57
download 20
downtown 39
drawing pin 28
dream 15
dressing gown 24
dressing table 24

sensible 2
sensitive 7
separate 16
serious 7
seriously 51
serve 31
set out 3
sew 49
sex 32
shampoo 21
shape 56
share 16
shaved 37
shoe polish 24
shoelace 24
shoplifting 8
shore 49
show off 3
side-parting 37
sidewalk 39
signature 32
silk 48
singer 31
sink 22
situation 30
ski stick 29
skills 13
sleeping bag 28
sleeve 25
slice 10
smart 59
smile 52
smooth 33
sneeze 15
snore 15
snorkel 29
so 49
solve 38
songs 31
speech therapist 9
speeding 8
speedometer 35
spoil 50
spoilt 26
sponge bag 21
sports car 44
spots 37
spread 10
squeeze 10
stairs 49

stale 55
stamp 56
stand in line 39
stare 49
starting salary 13
starving 45
status 32
stay up 26
steak 5
steep 55
steering wheel 35
sticky 55
stir 10
stomach 4
stone 55
stop 26
strap 25
strength 53
stressful 13
strict 19
string 18
strip light 18
stubble 37
study 52
submarine 44
subway 39
succeed 50
sudden 7
suitcase 1
sun cream 24
sunglasses 24
superficial 2
superstitious 41
support 11
suppose 38
sure 49
surgeon 9
surname 32
surveyor 31
swan 23
swap 50
sympathetic 19

T
table tennis bat 29
take away 31
take off 3
take up 46
talcum powder 21
talented 19

tangerine 12
tap 6
tarantula 23
tasty 59
tattoo 37
tea 5
tea towel 1
tease 38
telephone directory 24
telephone number 24
tell 60
tell off 3
temporary 13
terrify 38
theft 8
thermometer 18
thick-skinned 7
throat 4
thumb 4
tie 57
timetable 47
timid 19
tiny 7
tip 56
title 32
to 36
tomatoes 5
toothbrush 24
toothpaste 24
tortoise 23
tractor 44
traffic 54
train 22
training course 13
translate 14
trash 39
tray 1
treat 31
triangular 33
trust 38
tuna 23
turkey 23
turn down 46
turn up 3
twist 60
tyre 35

U
unattractive 17
under 43

Test Your way to success in English
Test Your Grammar and Skills

Verbs

0582 45176 0

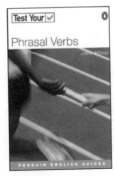

Phrasal Verbs

0582 45171 X

Prepositions

0582 45172 8

Idioms

0582 45173 6

Vocabulary for FCE

0582 45175 2

Grammar and Usage for FCE

0582 45174 4

Pronunciation

0582 46902 3

Listening

0582 46908 2

Reading

0582 46905 8

Test Your way to success in English

Test Your Professional English

0582 45163 9

0582 45148 5

0582 45149 3

0582 45160 4

0582 45161 2

0582 46898 1

0582 46897 3

0582 45150 7

0582 45147 7

0582 45162 0

www.penguinenglish.com